Touch Not My Anointed

And Do My Prophet No Harm

Ann C. Hutchinson

outskirtspress
DENVER, COLORADO

The opinions expressed in this manuscript are solely the opinions of the author and do not represent the opinions or thoughts of the publisher. The author has represented and warranted full ownership and/or legal right to publish all the materials in this book.

Touch Not My Anointed
And Do My Prophet No Harm
All Rights Reserved.
Copyright © 2015 Ann C. Hutchinson
v2.0

Cover Photo © 2015 thinkstockphotos.com. All rights reserved - used with permission.

This book may not be reproduced, transmitted, or stored in whole or in part by any means, including graphic, electronic, or mechanical without the express written consent of the publisher except in the case of brief quotations embodied in critical articles and reviews.

Outskirts Press, Inc.
http://www.outskirtspress.com

ISBN: 978-1-4787-5934-8

Outskirts Press and the "OP" logo are trademarks belonging to Outskirts Press, Inc.

PRINTED IN THE UNITED STATES OF AMERICA

The word of the LORD came to me, saying,
"Before I formed you in the womb I knew you,
before you were born I set you apart;
I appointed you as a prophet to the nations."

Jeremiah 1:4-5 (NIV)

To My Father Jesus

"Mission Accomplished"
With Gratefulness
If it were not for you, I would not be here today.
It was you and only you that gave me a reason
to live!

Also this book is dedicated to my husband, Larry.
You are truly a gift from God!
I love you more than words can say!

ACKNOWLEDGMENTS

First and foremost I would like to thank my God for making my life so rewarding, so fulfilling and so rich. I came to Michigan looking for love and I found it in Him. My God is so captivating, so mesmerizing and so hypnotic. He is now and always will be a major blessing in my life.

When God called me out and asked me to write this book, it touched me in a deep place for I knew that He would not have asked me to write had He not put in me the ability to do it. When God asks you to do something, He not only equips you but He also anoints you and empowers you and arranges the right people to help you. I would like to thank the people that I believe God put in my life to help me with this task. I would like to thank my sister, Freda Cox. You will always be my favorite sister! Thank you for your generosity. You have been more than a sister to me, you have been a great friend. Thank you "Prophet" Deborah Rose. I love you! You will always be my loving friend! You are a "Pearl of a great Price!"

I also would like to thank my beautiful "Sister in Christ" Wendy Zick. You will always be my most cherished friend! You are like a sister to me! I love you!

Pastor Dave, when I first came to church, you and Mary Jo gave me so much hope and encouragement, thank you!

I would like to thank my friend, Jeanette Howard, for her encouragement, inspiration and motivation. Thank you for pushing me to continue and challenging me to strive for more. What a valuable and faithful friend she was (deceased). Thank you, my friend and my spiritual brother, Tom Frankovich. You have always been and will always be a genuine friend!

Thank you, Barbara Williams, for being such a devoted and a loyal friend and a prayer partner for almost two years. Thank you, Mary Collins, for helping me with my book, and inspiring me to persevere. You, Mary are a rare jewel! I also would like to thank one amazing woman who helped me and encouraged me to continue my journey. Lady Katheryn Hamm. Lady Katheryn, thank you for reading my first draft and encouraging me to continue. You gave me Hope, more than you know!" There are three people in my life that have been a spiritual mom to me and I love them with all of my heart. I can honestly say that they changed my life and I look up to them as if they were my real moms! Nan O'Meara, Mariam Riddle and Mary Mooney, I love you!

Thank you, Katie Velez, for being a good friend when I needed someone to lean on. I love you, my sister! I would like to thank Peter Higbie for being there from the beginning of my journey. Your guidance and support meant so much to me. You are a treasure! I would like to also thank my niece, "Dr. Octavia Cannon." I lived with her and her parents (My brother Harvey and his wife Roberta) for a while when I first came to Michigan and I grew to love Tay like she was my own daughter. Now, she is a doctor in North Carolina and I still think of her like a little girl. Later on in life I got to know her younger sister, Rita, and I love her also. I am sooo glad you ladies are in my life, thank you!

Last but not least, I would like to thank my very best friend and my husband, Larry M. Hutchinson. There are no words to describe the love and the gratitude I have for you. You have not only helped me with my book, but you are helping me with my life. Larry M. Hutchinson, thank you, I love you!

FOREWORD

Reading Ann's book, I'm impressed by it. Ann is a humble woman and I know that her intent is not to impress people. But I am deeply impressed. I'm impressed by the depth and power of her connection to God. I'm impressed by how far away I am from having that kind of relationship with Him. Her descriptions make me yearn to draw nearer, much nearer to Him. I believe that's why God wanted Ann to write this book. He wants people to have insight into the kind of intimate relationship He's looking for with His beloved people.

If a prophet's purpose is to convey what is in God's heart to his people, then this is a prophetic work of the highest order. I believe that the greatest desire in God's heart is to have a close bond, an intimate connection with us, His children. He yearns to have us draw near and cry out to Him from a heart of love. He aches to reach out to us and whisper in our ears about how much He loves us.

This book is deeply painful, and joyful, and honest. And I believe there is an anointing on this book. I also believe that the anointing will fall upon many who read it. Don't be surprised if you find a growing fire inside of you, and a growing desire to spend time with the Lord.

Larry M. Hutchinson

TABLE OF CONTENTS

Introduction/Ordained by God 1
What is the Anointing? 14
God's Chosen Remnants 18
Confirmations 23
A Word Given 30
Opposition 39
A Secret Between You And Me 58
Driven by Love 63
A Child Of Dreams 69
The Strange One 83
God heals 92
Prophets 97
The Visitor 107
That Secret Place 113
Reckless Abandonement 126
Touch Not My Anointed 139
Ann's History 148
"But In My Sin, God Still Loved Me." 151
A Moment Of Clarity 167
A God Encounter 174
Tears Of Deep Sadness 178

Plague Of Flies	180
Prayer Of Salvation	184
Miracles, Signs, And Wonders	190
The Epitome of Evil	196
A Word From God	204
Handprint Of The Enemy	208
The High Point Of My Life	212
Titanic/America	215
Lion Of Judah	238
Ordinary People	245
Dreams And Visions	249
A Misfit To Men, But by God's Standard, A Giant In The Eyes Of Heaven.	260
Submit to God and you will have peace	274
Ann's prayer To the Almighty	275

INTRODUCTION/ORDAINED BY GOD

John 15:16 New King James Version (NKJV)

[16] You did not choose me, but I chose you and appointed you that you should go and bear fruit, and *that* your fruit should remain, that whatever you ask the Father in My name He may give you.

You are probably wondering where I came up with that title. To be honest with you, it was not my idea. I believe with every fiber of my being that it was God's idea. I could never have come up with a title such as this one on my own.

One morning while I was on my knees praying to God, I believe that He asked me to write a book. I proceeded to ask Him about the title and all I heard was His silence. As I was meditating on His word, I heard someone say "Touch Not my Anointed." I usually keep Christian music playing in the background in my home all during the day so I immediately went to the CD player. I was listening to see if there was a slight possibility "Touch not my anointed" was somewhere in one of the songs I was playing. However, I played the songs over and over again and finally I was fully convinced that the words "touch not my anointed" was not on this CD. I exhausted every avenue and then it hit me all at once like nothing ever hit me before, like a tidal wave!! I paused for a moment to carefully consider that maybe it is a slight possibility, a slight possibility that it was God's voice I heard, answering my prayer! Once again, I was amazed and intrigued and amused with my father, still trying to figure Him out! In His word to Jeremiah (33:3, NKJV) He said, "Call to me and I will answer you and I will show you great and mighty things!"

Consider this: I called to God and asked Him if He wanted me to write a book, and if He did, what would my title be? When He did answer me, I did not even recognize His voice. Again, consider this—I asked God a question and when He answered me, I tried to figure out where the answer came from. It was so clear. "Touch Not My Anointed"! It made me wonder all the more if I was actually expecting Him to answer me in the first place. I was torn between two impulses: the urge to pretend I did not hear what I thought I heard, or just to get on my knees and seek God further concerning this title.

At this point, I could not think straight, my heart was pounding and my whole body was shaking. I was captivated and mesmerized and spellbound by what I thought I heard! I could not comprehend or even process the thought of writing such a book. Nevertheless, I knew this was not about the messenger, it was about the message. It was about God! I finally settled down but all I could think about was writing this book.

Day after day and night after night I knew deep down inside that it was time for my book to be written. It was time for this message to be given! It was time for an unyielding devotion

INTRODUCTION/ORDAINED BY GOD

to writing this book! I paused to carefully consider this huge undertaking. I know that this is the appointed time for it to go forth and let the whole world know that God still speaks to His people. Days went by and even weeks. I could not even sleep. All I could think about was the voice of God speaking to me and it was almost impossible for me to concentrate on anything else. One day as I was praying to God, I paused for a moment to carefully consider who I am; and then it hit me, all at once, like a ton of bricks. I believe that I am unique and chosen, that even as a baby I was dedicated and conceived for the purpose of the will of God, like Israel, and also like America. In Deuteronomy 7:6—NIV—God said this to His people, Israel:

"For you are a people Holy to the Lord your God. The Lord your God has chosen you out of all the peoples on the face of the earth to be His people, "His Treasured Possession."

One day I was thinking about writing this book and I could not imagine even doing it, so I began praying to God and I asked Him to help me because I loved Him and I am devoted to Him and my one and only desire is to please Him and Him alone! In any case all I heard was His silence. Suddenly, I heard these words in my heart:

"Ann, as I love Israel as my special possession, I love you!" He went on to say that His love for me is strong and passionate and that He is consumed with love for me. In a small still voice, He said that He (Himself) will help me write His Book.

Once again I paused for a moment, slowly, cautiously and carefully deliberating every word that I heard in my heart and then I realized, more than I had realized before that these words were not my words at all but they were God's. His words were like fire, piercing every part of my being. My heart began to race with excitement and I could not think straight nor process what I believe my Father in heaven revealed to me. And then it hit me that God loves me as He loves His firstborn Israel and He has a plan for me just as He has plans for Israel. I then got up from praying and I had such joy in my heart and everything that was bothering me suddenly left without warning. I was free from the burden of having to write this book alone. I knew without a shadow of a doubt that God was going to help me. It was an "aha" moment and my heart was pleased!

In any event, I began to speak out loud as if I was recalling a distant memory. When I was small, I would often see a vision of a tablet and a pen and I did not understand what it meant, but somehow I believed it was a foreshadowing of something very significant.

But who would have known that vision was not only a mystery but it was a message of great importance that held the key to my future. I did not know it back then but I know it now that I am going to be a writer, proclaiming the word of God and God (Himself) is going to help me! In fact, I believe that I was wired by God to write before I was formed in my mom's womb and that is why I would see these visions.

INTRODUCTION/ORDAINED BY GOD

I remember thinking in my heart as a young girl that wherever there is a vision, there is a message. I had no idea where that thought came from. Nevertheless, I was torn between two impulses—the urge to tell my mom about it or just ponder it in my heart.

Eventually, I made a decision to keep it to myself and ponder it in my heart like Mary in the Bible when she had a visitation from heaven! Somehow I could not imagine my mom understanding any of it. However, I believe with all of my heart that I was predestined by God to write and now it is the appropriate appointed time for me to do it. As I finished praying and thoughts ran through my head, I paused to carefully consider how God and I were going to carry out this task. I am not much of a reader and based on what I know, writers are readers. Good writers are very expressive and very good with words. I don't consider myself to be either. So I realized that I would have to trust God and He would definitely be the one who gave this message and I was the messenger! There is one thing I do know and that is when God calls you to do anything, He will first anoint you and equip you and appoint you for that task. He will even line up the right people and put the right opportunity in place to help you. I believe that I am ready to write, I believe that I am ready to be anointed with the gift of words, with the help of my father, the King, the Master Writer, The Master Storyteller!

In any event, this title "Touch Not My Anointed, And Do

My Prophet No Harm" was His choice and this is His Book. It is not about me but it is about the one who sent me.

Let's get started!!

In the fall of 2011, I went to a meeting in Florida with a group of people from my church. It was the Increase Event with Bob Harrison and Myles Munroe. After the meeting let out on the last day, my friend Jeanette Howard said she wanted to receive a prophetic word from Myles Munroe. Myles Munroe is a pastor in the Bahamas and a motivational speaker. He is the author and coauthor of over 100 books.

Jeanette said, "Ann, let's go over and have him prophesy over us." We looked at one another and we both went over to where he was standing. She went up to him first. When she was finished, I went up. He looked at me and asked what I would like for him to pray about. I told him that I was in the process of writing a book and I wanted him to bless it and I asked him to pray that it will be successful. He looked at me and paused for a moment to carefully consider what he was about to say. He said that I was not only going to write one book but "you are going to write seven books." He then told me that each one would sell a million copies. Then he said the same anointing that he had when he wrote his books would be imparted to me. He reached out and hugged me tightly and prayed over me. Then he said he was going to blow on me. When he blew his breath, I felt like he was breathing life into the impartation that he spoke.

INTRODUCTION/ORDAINED BY GOD

Job 33:4 NIV—says "The spirit of God hath made me, and the breath of the Almighty hath given me life."

I was numb! I did not know what to say or what to do and I just gazed at Myles Munroe trying to absorb what he said to me because it was a lot to take in. Nevertheless, I thanked him and said, "Let it be done to me according to your word." The words that He spoke over me lightened the load, healed my heart and strengthened my spirit and somewhat lifted the burden of writing these books alone.

However, I was still caught up in the mystery, trying with all my heart to digest it all. I kept thinking in my head "seven books?" The whole thing just did not seem real! Meanwhile I was torn between two impulses—how was I going to write seven books when I have not even written one. I was intrigued and excited yet at the same time I was somewhat overwhelmed and apprehensive that it would not happen. Although I knew that God would help me, I was still afraid!

Nevertheless, I let him (Myles Monroe) know that I was in full agreement, although I was basically in shock, even frozen. I thought I was going to write one book, but he said that I would write seven and they all would sell a million copies? Wow, God is so good! In 1 Cor. 2:9 it reads-But it is written, "Eye hath not seen, nor ear heard, neither have entered into the heart of man, the things which God hath prepared for them who love Him."

TOUCH NOT MY ANOINTED

I believe it was God (Himself) that spoke to Myles Munroe concerning me writing seven books. Unfortunately, Myles Munroe and his wife were killed in an airplane crash this year, 2015, but His life still lives on in heaven with God and on earth through his many books! I was soo sad when I heard the news. Although we know heaven is his eternal home, it does not make it any easier for those who are left behind. He will be forever missed!

You see, in 2011 when Myles Munroe prophesied over me I believe that God put me in the right place at the right time and He provided the right person to speak in my life prophesying what He had already spoken to me. However, I had no idea that I would be writing that many books! God is all about making us 1000 times more than what we expect. In any event, I did not know what to think about writing that many books, considering that writing a first book is not an easy task to accomplish. To be honest with you, as you may have guessed, I did not know how to take this. I was excited and amused but totally baffled. The thought of writing seven books was at first not even a slight possibility. Nevertheless, when I do write that many books, this would be nothing short of a miracle.

In spite of what I was feeling, I knew deep within me the key to my writing these books would mean that I will need to cultivate a greater intimacy with the king and at the right time, seven books will come.

I will never forget this event in Florida! It really has changed

INTRODUCTION/ORDAINED BY GOD

my life. Not only has it changed my life, but it has changed my perspective of thinking "Big" and living outside the box and seeing beyond normal sight.

As I write my first book, I write about some of the people in the Bible that were anointed by God and were living outside the box and seeing beyond what the natural eye can see. Not only do I write about them, I also share with you a glimpse of my life and how God speaks to me and protects me, for I am one of His anointed!

Recently, I was driving down the highway and all of a sudden a small fast-driving car pulled up in front of me and cut me off. I put my foot on the brake to keep from hitting him. I was almost to the point of pulling over to the side of the road to try to calm myself down, and out of the blue, a huge black truck pulled up in front of this same car and cut him off and almost ran him off the road. It was as if this truck appeared out of nowhere, and I know the driver in the small car was in shock. Suddenly, the man in the small car slowed down as if he did not know what just happened. In the meantime, I pulled in front of him due to the fact that he had slowed down way below the normal speed limit. I looked to see if he was ok, but he was so baffled and so shaken that he could hardly drive. As I passed him, I could almost read what he was thinking! He looked over at me with fear in his eyes. I could almost sense that his heart was pounding and he could not process what just happened!! I believe that it was God's way of saying to this driver, "Do not mess with my anointed one." (I do not want you to think that

◄ TOUCH NOT MY ANOINTED

I am bragging but this is not a rare occurrence; God protects me and He always fights my battles!)

I pray that this driver learned his lesson and I believe that now as a result of what happened, that he believes life is not all about him but it is about the one who created Him. I do not know who this man is, but I will continue to pray for him. I believe that God is after his heart.

Nevertheless, when I arrived home, I paused for a moment to consider how the God of the universe is on my side and I began to worship Him.

God said, "Touch not my anointed and do my prophets no harm."

1 Chronicles 16:22 –"God protects His anointed ones."

God protected me and He fought my battle! How awesome is that! In Hebrews chapter 10:30a and verse 31 (NLT) "I will take revenge, I will pay them back. It's a terrible thing to fall into the hands of a living God."

Most of my life, I have heard from God. He has revealed many things to me through dreams and visions and signs and wonders. Even when I did not know Him, I believed that I heard from Him.

"Hear now my words: If there is a prophet among you, I, the Lord, make it known to him in a vision; I speak to him in a dream" Numbers 12:6 NKJV.

INTRODUCTION/ORDAINED BY GOD

"I have also spoken by the prophets, and have multiplied visions; I have given symbols through the witness of prophets" Hosea 12:10, NKJV.

I would say that these dreams have even guided my life. Some of these dreams were and still are prophetic messages of correction, warnings, I believe to save people, and to save me from calamity. Some of these dreams and visions are even showing me my future. I have learned that God not only speaks to us in His word and through the prompting of the Holy Spirit and through people, but He sometimes shows us His perfect and good will for our lives through dreams and visions.

I once read a book called Dream Interpretation by Herman Riffle. In this book it said that when Albert Einstein was asked where his theory of relativity had originated, he attributed it to a dream he experienced in his youth. According to the story, he was riding in a sled which started going faster and faster until it approached the speed of light, at which time the stars broke into fantastic colors. He said that the rest of his life was a meditation on that dream. In any case, I believe that God had given him a clear vision of the thoughts of his own heart and the consequences of allowing those thoughts to guide his life. I may be wrong, but I believe when Albert Einstein was young, somewhere deep within his heart, he had a desire to explore the theory of relativity, and God challenged those desires through his dream. How awesome is that!

◄ TOUCH NOT MY ANOINTED

I am not sure, but I have a good idea why God talks to me through dreams and visions. Maybe it is because it is hard for me to hear His voice, or maybe it is because when I am awake I am more distracted.

As you read on, you will see how God would give me prophetic dreams and visions even as a child as he did with Albert Einstein, to somehow prepare me for my prophetic future. God's voice will be heard, whether you listen to Him or not.

I believe that you will enjoy this true story of Dreams and Visions and prophecy of "Touch Not God's Anointed."

In the Bible, the prophets would receive a word through dreams and visions and impartations, and then these prophets would be responsible to deliver the word to a nation or to individuals either by proclaiming it or putting it in writing as I am doing.

Unfortunately, for a long time God was giving me dreams and visions and when I proclaimed it to the people who were over me, they would reject it. I did not have the courage to take a stand so I bowed down to their pressure and was molded to be just like them because I wanted to be normal and fit in. However, later on I realized that because I was trying to fit in, it neutralized my position and it delayed my progress. What a terrible mistake! Beloved, based on my experience, if God gives you a word, no matter how much you have to suffer, stand by His

INTRODUCTION/ORDAINED BY GOD

word and proclaim it and He will always be there to help you and to defend you! I realize that in order to lay hold of the finished work of Jesus Christ, you have to be fearless in the face of opposition, and fearless in the face of difficulty, hardship, and pain and stand your ground no matter what! It really does take courage to take a stand! However, I have learned from my mistakes.

Meanwhile, check out the Book of Jeremiah and Book of Isaiah and many other biblical prophets who actually listened to God and obeyed Him!

I pray that as you read, the Holy Spirit will come upon you and you yourself will be touched by the anointing.

Revelation 12:11—(NKJV)-"And they overcame him by the blood of the Lamb and by the word of their testimony and they did not love their lives to the death."

Beloved, something powerful happens when you share your testimony; better yet, when you hear someone's testimony, it gives you hope and it also seems to unlock people's faith! God loves to redeem our story to help other people.

Sit back now and enjoy "Touch Not My Anointed."

WHAT IS THE ANOINTING?

I would like to explain the meaning of anointing or the anointed. The Webster's Collegiate Dictionary's definition says that to anoint is to apply oil as a sacred ritual for consecration, to designate as if by a ritual anointment. The Bible Dictionary says the anointing was and is a means of investing someone with power, such as the anointing of King Solomon in the Bible upon his ascent to the throne (1King 1:39), perhaps to signify divine sanctification and approval. It could also signify the consecration of someone or something for a Holy purpose. Jacob in (Gen. 28:18) anointed a pillar at Bethel, calling this place a house of God. Other Scripture references concerning the anointing are as follows. Aaron was anointed for the priesthood (Exodus 29:7). In Acts 10:38, Peter testified regarding how God anointed Jesus of Nazareth with the Holy Spirit.

Anointing could be with oil (Old Testament and The New Testament) as part of a ritual, or it can be a touch of empowerment by God Himself. The anointing is not just for the Old Testament and the New, it is for such a time as this. It is for the "Now." The anointing brings healing, deliverance, restoration and it brings you out of depression. The anointing of the Lord will take you from the valley to the top of the mountain and it will give you lasting fruit. When the anointing comes upon you, your faith will be empowered and come alive and the words you speak will

WHAT IS THE ANOINTING?

bring forth lasting results. Last but not least, when you have an anointing on your life, it can take an ordinary man and turn him to an extraordinary man who will do extraordinary work.

One day I was on the floor praying. I was lying out before the Lord, desperate to hear a word from God. Suddenly the anointing of the Lord came upon me and I asked God what my purpose is and where I am in reference to fulfilling it and I also asked Him, "Father , please give me the sequence of what I need to do and where am I supposed to be in order to fulfill it." I believe the word of the Lord came to me and it was burning in me so strong, I knew it was from Him.

"Ann, I will take a tender sprout from the top of a tall cedar and I will plant it on top of Israel's highest mountain. It shall become a noble cedar, bringing forth branches and bearing seed. Animals of every sort will gather under it; its branches will shelter every kind of bird. And everyone shall know that it is I, the Lord, who cuts down the high trees and exalts the low, that I make the green tree wither and the dead tree grow. I, the Lord, have said that I would do it, and I will" (Ezekiel 17:22-24) One Year Bible-NLT.

And then I believe that I heard Him say—"Ann, you are, at this time, the tender sprout that I will be using. I have a plan for you. I will make you into a noble cedar, bringing forth branches and bearing seed. I, the Lord, who cuts down the high trees and exalts the low, and makes the

green tree wither and the dead tree grow. I, the Lord have said that I would do it, and I will.

I paused for a moment and pondered that word in my heart, slowly, cautiously, and carefully examining every word. I meditated on it day after day and incubated it in my head and in my heart until it began to speak to me. I then asked God once again, "Where am I, Lord, in reference to the fulfillment of this prophecy; and God, what is the process to allow me to fulfill these words so I can step into the identity to become the person you saw when you spoke it?" As I waited for Him to answer me, my heart was pounding, waiting in expectation of His response. I waited and waited but He did not answer me. I was beginning to grow weary and then the word of the Lord came to me weeks later.

In Jeremiah:

"For I know the thoughts that I think toward you," says the Lord, *"thoughts of peace and not of evil to give you a future and a hope. Then you will call on me and come and pray to me, and I will listen to you"* Jeremiah 29:11-12—(NKJV).

The word of the Lord came to me saying,

"Before I formed you in the womb I knew you, before you were born I set you apart; I appointed you as a prophet to the nations" Jeremiah 1:4-5 (NIV).

WHAT IS THE ANOINTING?

I felt like God was saying to me, and I almost hesitate to say this, that He had called me to be one of His prophets. I told God that I could not speak and would not know what to say nor what to do. I also told Him that I was not smart and I did not have a title beside my name and that no one would listen to me; and without a beat, I believe that He said that He would listen to me! I also believe that He went on to say that I would be perfect as one of His prophets and that He (Himself) would give me a voice, a voice that no one can dissipate! Suddenly, it hit me like a ton of bricks, all at once that God is calling not only me but all of His children to see the invisible and achieve the impossible! The only way we will be able to do that is to seize the moment, to sail against the wind, to swim against the tide and go against the odds and really put our trust in Him!

GOD'S CHOSEN REMNANTS

I believed with all of my heart that God said that He is raising up a remnant (fragment-trace-remainder-trophy-keepsake-token). These remnants would be free from the burden of false pretense, and free from the burden of offending people and being offended. I believe that these remnants will be "the Emerging Leaders" of our times. I read this book by Pastor David Williams. It is called "Emerging Leaders." In this book, he said that the "Emerging Leaders will be a new breed of Church Leadership for the 21st Century." According to him, they will often be unorthodox in their approach; and don't try to understand them and don't try to figure them out because they will be different."

I believe the word that God spoke to me when I was meditating refers to the same people that Pastor Dave wrote about in his book. However, Pastor Dave called them the 'emerging leaders' and the name that I believe God gave me was "remnants." In any case, I believe that they are one and the same.

I believed that God told me concerning these remnants, that no army can defeat them. No force on earth is more powerful than these remnants. I believed He said that they would have the spirit of Elijah. Read about Elijah (1 & 2 Kings)

GOD'S CHOSEN REMNANTS

Why? I believe that God has set them apart from the world and consecrated them unto Himself even before they were formed in their mom's womb. These remnants will hear the voice of God and act on His Word quickly. They will not have the fear of man but will have the fear of God and God alone. I also believe that most of these remnants are going to be misunderstood, mistreated, underestimated and sometimes rejected because of their deep desire to please the Lord as opposed to pleasing man.

However, I believe that anyone who mistreats God's anointed will get God's attention and He will not take it likely and is going to act quickly on their behalf. "Touch Not My Anointed and do my Prophet no harm."

These remnants are going to be empowered by God. God is going to equip them and appoint them and anoint them to do the work for His Kingdom. As I continued to meditate and listen to what I believe God was speaking to my heart, I became excited for I knew that He is preparing His army at this very moment and again, I hesitate to say this, but I sensed that I am a part of it and I am one of them. There is a song, I can't seem to remember the title or who wrote it, but I believe it says that "there is an army that is rising up" and I believe wholeheartedly that this army will be God's remnants, God's chosen few.

The word of the Lord clearly came to me and I believed that I immediately had a confirmation. I believe that He said that I was part of His latter day remnants and He wanted me to pray for them. I believed that He asked me to pray for them diligently. This is what I believed God was saying to me:

"Ann, remind me of my promises. Do not be silent, and do not give me rest until the promises you are praying about these remnants come to past."

I believe that He also told me that some of these remnants would be old and some would be as young as six years old. So I began to pray for His Army:

"Father, I am reminding you of your promises concerning raising up remnants for these end times. Father, I ask that you open the eyes of your chosen remnants' understanding. Let them see what you want them to see and let them respond according to your Word. I pray at this very moment, Father, that you will let your spirit brood over them like a raging flood, creating a thirst and a hunger and a craving and a desire for you like never before. Cause your remnants to have a deeper more intimate and more passionate relationship with you. Intoxicate them with your presence. Inspire them to talk like you, walk like you, and respond like you. Most of all, Father, enable them (us) to love like you beyond their own ability. I bind deception and I lose your truth. Let your truth by-pass the head and go directly to their heart and there will be a heart change. I release the spirit of truth over your remnants Lord and I release the spirit of love. Father, I pray that they have eyes to see and ears to hear and a heart to obey, In Jesus' name I pray, Amen."

After I prayed the prayer over God's chosen, (including myself) I was not sure what part God wanted me to play in raising up these remnants besides praying for them. However, I do know one thing and that is, God is calling me to step out of the boat and walk on water, not knowing where I am going, except that He is leading me there.

It is almost like walking in a fog, but holding God's hand.

The fact that I do not know where He is taking me tells me that God is unpredictable, but also very consistent.

The way that I felt about this reminded me of Moses in the Bible when God asked him to speak to Pharaoh concerning freeing His people. Moses said that he could not do this because he stuttered. He believed he was not up to this challenge. I felt the same way. I kept trying to convince God that He could find someone who was more secure and better qualified in fulfilling this purpose. I told Him that I had so many imperfections, flaws, and blemishes. I also reminded Him of many mistakes that I had made in my life. However, I knew that these things would not disqualify me for the call that He has on my life.

I also told God that being one of His remnants (a prophet) seems like more than I could handle. He repeated to me that I was one of His chosen remnants.

Once again, I believed that He said that I was perfect. The fact that He thought that I was perfect flooded my heart with joy, filling my expectation with hope and preparing the way for a new beginning. I knew that it was time for me to constantly read His Word to renew my mind and meditate and incubate it for weeks, maybe even months or even for years! However, I was still not fully persuaded that I would be His best choice.

I asked God, "Who am I to be one of your prophets? I kept asking Him, why me? He responded, "Why not you? You are so right for me."

CONFIRMATIONS

In any event, a week later the Lord gave me a confirmation. I believe it was at the Sunday night service at my local church. My former pastor was at the opposite end of the room. He said that he was under the anointing and he believed God was speaking to him about me. He walked over to where I was sitting. As a result of him being empowered by the Holy Spirit, he singled me out and gave me a prophetic word about the anointing that God was giving me.

My pastor said that I was going to come into the prophetic realm and I would flow in the gift of prophecy.

I usually do not cry easily, but the tears flowed out of my eyes and they would not stop coming. My heart was touched and I was deeply moved. I have never felt more valuable than I felt at that very moment. Suddenly, my mindset shifted and I knew the call on my life was real. In any case, I realized that we are sometimes shaped by circumstance and often we are shaped by what people say. My thinking was never the same after that. Those few words changed my life and I was deeply touched by the power of the anointing. Then it hit me all at once that this was a confirmation of what my Father had already told me!

I had not shared with my pastor nor anyone else what God had revealed to me a week prior, regarding the Prophetic

Anointing. God revealed to my pastor things about my future through the anointing. In any event, I held on to those encouraging and prophetic words and I pondered it in my heart and I received this prophetic word from the Lord. I said, "Let it be done, Lord, according to your word."

I believed with all of my heart that someday that prophecy would come to pass.

My former pastor may not know it, but I believe that he also is one of God's greatest prophets. When God handed out the gifts, I believe that he was given more than his share of them. He, in my opinion, is brilliant. However, his gifts pale compared to God's.

This bears repeating, I was amazed that my pastor confirmed to me what God had already told me. What an awesome God!!! What an obedient pastor!!

In God's word, He said a word fitly spoken is like apples of gold in settings of silver. Proverbs 25:11 (NKJV).

My spirit leaped when he was speaking over me as if my spirit was bearing witness to the truth.

Tears flowed out of my eyes like rivers of living water. I was torn between two impulses. I felt a sense of relief but on the other hand, a little frightened that I would disappoint my God. All I knew was, this is the fingerprint of the one who sent it, a message directly from God Almighty!

I remember as if it was yesterday, after the service was over, my friend, Jeanette Howard, came running over to me and asked me if I wrote down what the pastor had said. She was so excited for me. Actually, she seemed more excited than me. I looked at her and I did not know what to say, so I said nothing. I think my tears spoke for me!

I was numb and yet my heart was pounding. I could not think straight and I could not process what I heard. The tears were still flowing, for I knew even as a child, I was hearing from God (although I did not know Him). However, I somehow believed that He had a huge call on my life and I knew deep down inside that I would, in due season, if I kept my eyes on Him, come into the fullness of my purpose. In any event, I believe that purpose has now come upon me and it is time for His message to be given and His words to be proclaimed.

Within minutes this verse came to me. "Hope deferred makes the heart sick but when it comes, it is like a tree of life" Proverbs 13:12 (NJKV).

From that day on, I was filled with encouragement and hope; but my hope turned into searching and seeking what I needed to do next. At one point I realized that it is the glory of God to conceal a matter and the honor of kings is to seek it out. I sought out prophets and read up on every prophet I could find. I searched for common ground and I found many cases of it. I studied and studied and the more I studied about prophets and their characteristics, I began to realize that God had called me to do this. I was finally willing and ready to accept the challenge, although I still had some reservations.

The challenge was definitely something that was far beyond my reach. I knew that I could not do this without the help of God. I cried for many days but wasn't sure why. Was it happy tears or was it tears of fear? Although I felt like I was up for the challenge, I knew that I needed God's anointing to accomplish this task. Without God, I could not do it and I did not even know if I wanted to.

As time went by, I felt like God was speaking more and more and I was listening. I believed that God spoke to me through His Word, through other believers, and through my pastor. I would pray to God about something and the following Sunday, my former pastor would answer my prayer. Still other times, I would ask God a question and I would go sit at the table and a handwritten note (it looked like my handwriting) would just appear on the table answering my prayer. I had no idea where the note came from and I do not remember even writing it.

Sometime later, a well—known healing evangelist came to our church. I will just call him Pastor Billy. He is an author, teacher, evangelist; and I believe that he is also a prophet. One night he was ministering healing to the people at our church and after he left the sanctuary, my friend, Deb, and I left right after he did. I remember being so tired because we were there late into the night. My focus was on going home and getting some sleep. However, after leaving the sanctuary I heard a voice say, "Wow! Look at all that power." I turned and saw the evangelist walking up to Deb and I and he touched my head and immediately I went down under the power of the Holy Spirit. Deb said that he asked her to help me up when I was ready to get up. I eventually got up with help from Deb and she explained to me what had just happened. She said after we left the sanctuary, she saw the evangelist looking right at me. As he walked toward me, he began to speak saying, "Look at that power on that lady." He proceeded to walk toward me and he touched me and the Spirit of the Lord came upon me all at once like a ton of bricks and I immediately went down under the power. I remember it as if it was yesterday.

When I first awoke from falling down under the power, the fire that came upon me was like fire caught up in my bones.

It was so powerful, I almost could not contain it!

I began to feel weary from holding it in. I did not know what to do. I did not know what to say. It was like nothing I had ever felt in my whole life. It was a high beyond my wildest imagination. I felt so drunk in the Spirit as if I had stepped out of the natural and stepped into the supernatural, and stepped out of the ordinary into the extraordinary! When I was slain in the spirit, I do not remember whether or not I was unconscious, semi-conscious or fully conscious. However, I do remember one thing: it was a powerful move of God!!

Eventually, after I got up, I walked out of the building and got into my car and drove home. I do not remember even driving.

When I arrived home a word from the Lord came to me,

"I am with you like a mighty warrior and your persecutors will stumble and fall. Ann, I have called you to speak to my people and if they reject you, it is not you they are rejecting, they are rejecting me. I am the Lord Thy God."

My voice, almost shaking, was filled with intensity and I responded "Let it be done unto me according to your word."

I realized I had another confirmation and it was from God Almighty. At this point I was intrigued and amused. I kept meditating on His Word, slowly, cautiously and carefully deliberating every word. I was chewing on His Word like chewing on good food.

As time passed Pastor Billy came back to our church again to minister and pray for healings.

That night at the end of the impartation, I was sitting close to the front. He walked over to where I was sitting. He spoke a word to the congregation and he looked directly at me saying,

"So go and work on being a prophet."

I repeat, he looked directly at me and said that prophecy. You have to realize that I really had not talked to this evangelist before, but it was as if He was speaking specifically to me.

I said, "Lord, let it be done according to your word." I then began to ponder it in my heart. From that day forward I meditated on that word day and night and night and day. I pondered his words in my heart and I asked God to help me.

A WORD GIVEN

I know now what my calling is but am I comfortable with it? If not now, I will be. You may not believe me, but I am telling the truth. I am realizing for the first time in my life and at this very moment that God (Himself) has called me to be a prophet for such a time as this. I have had so many words from God telling me who I am in Him and He has even sent me so many confirmations and yet I have not been fully persuaded until today. In any case, it is time for God's Word to go forward. How could I have been so blind and so hard of hearing that I could have missed what He has been telling me for many years?

As I am writing, I believe that God has led me to this verse:

"Ann, do not forget this! Keep this in mind. 'Remember the things I have done in the past. For I alone am God. I am God and there is none like me. Only I can tell you the future before it even happens. Everything I plan will come to pass for I do whatever I wish. I have said what I would do and I will do it'" Isaiah 46:9-10 (NLT).

Do not get me wrong, I have not totally been in the dark but I have not been fully persuaded either until this very day. Again, I say that it is time for the word to be given and the message to be revealed!

A WORD GIVEN

I believe that God has sent me to speak on His behalf to be a witness and to be His servant as a prophet, and I am up to this challenge.

In Galatians 1:1 (NIV) it says: "Paul, an Apostle—sent not by men nor man, but by Jesus Christ and God the Father."

Apostle Paul was sent by God and He wrote over half of the New Testament. I also believe that I have been sent by God. It goes without saying that God specializes in creating something out of nothing.

Recently, I had a dream. I was walking down the street with my baby and I was holding her in my arms. Suddenly, I noticed a pack of wolves (or maybe they were dogs, I am not sure) running toward me. When I realized that they were running after me, I began to run as fast as I could and I did not look back. All I could think about was protecting my baby. My baby was my number one focus and I began to hold on to her so tight and I ran even faster. No matter what happens, I thought to myself, I was not going to let her go. All of a sudden, I noticed the wolves had caught up to me and one wolf jumped up at me and tried to close my mouth. His concern was not my baby, but it seemed he was more concerned about stopping what I had to say. He was trying to shut me up. Suddenly I awakened from the dream and I was puzzled as to what it meant. My heart was pounding and I could not think straight. I could not compute in my head what this dream meant. I was *torn between two impulses—the*

◄ TOUCH NOT MY ANOINTED

urge to keep this dream to myself and pray about it, or tell someone who might interpret exactly what this dream meant.

Suddenly, I realized that this dream was not only a mystery but it was a message, a prophecy of my future. I believed a mystery would be later revealed and a word would be given at an appointed time. However, every day I kept asking God what was He trying to say to me and I would get no response. I even mentioned it to some people at the church and they prayed over me.

Several weeks later, I was sitting at my desk at home. I noticed that there was a notebook beside my computer. I immediately glanced at the open page that was in front of me and I began to read it. To my amazement, I believed that God had answered my prayer concerning the dream. This is what the note said:

"God wants you to talk and not listen to those voices who are trying to shut you up. When the world around you says be silent, God says: I'm going to give you a voice."

First of all, I do not know where this notebook came from or how it found its way next to my computer at my desk at home. It was my handwriting but I do not remember writing it. In any case, I realized that now is the appointed time for the mystery to be revealed and the message to be given. One night I got on my knees and I asked God who are the wolves represented in my dream and why are they

A WORD GIVEN

trying to stop me from giving your message and speaking your truth? Who would want to do that?

Like Joseph in the Bible, I believe God was revealing to me in this dream my future. From that day on, I made a vow to God. I promised myself and God that when He speaks to me about any given situation, I will not allow myself to be squeezed into other people's mode and bow down to their pressure. I will take a stand and I shall not be moved!! It goes without saying that God believes that I have something to say and no one will be able to shut me up. I believe that God will protect me.

I believe that the baby was my ministry (prophetic ministry) and the wolves or dogs represented the enemy trying to stop my voice from proclaiming God's truth. The devil may sometimes succeed in delay, but he cannot succeed in denying what God has for you.

However, recently I was listening to Perry Stone on Mega Fest and He gave a biblical interpretation of what he believed that wolves represented. I truly believe it was God who had me to be watching Perry Stone so I would no longer be in the dark concerning my dream. He said that wolves represent hypocrites. Wow, that was an eye opener!! I had a question and I asked God, Who are the hypocrites that are trying to shut me up? I looked up hypocrites in the dictionary.com. It says:

Hypocrites—A person or persons who pretend to have

◄ TOUCH NOT MY ANOINTED

virtues, moral or religious beliefs, principles and etc. that he or she does not actually possess, especially a person or persons whose actions misrepresent stated beliefs. Also in the Bible, Jesus called the Pharisees hypocrites because they do things to be noticed by men and not BY God (Look up Matthew 23:5).

First of all, when Perry Stone said that wolves represented hypocrites, I was in deep sadness. When I looked up the word and it said that hypocrites are people who claim to be one thing and their life proves another. Wow, I could not make sense of it and again I was torn between two impulses—the urge to run as fast as I could or continue to seek God for wisdom. I chose to continue to seek God for more wisdom. I prayed and prayed for God to give me revelation and one day a word came.

"I know all the things you do, and I have opened a door for you that no one can close. You have little strength, yet you obeyed my word and did not deny me. Look, I will force those who belong to Satan's synagogue—those liars who say they are Jews but are not come and bow down at your feet. They will acknowledge that you are the ones I love." I looked this word up and I found it in Revelation 3:8-9 (NLT).

I also believed that God said,

"I will take revenge. I will pay them back, and I will judge my own people." It is a terrible thing to fall into the hands of the living God."

A WORD GIVEN

My heart was pounding and again I could not think straight, my hands were sweating and I could not process what I believe that the Living God was saying to me. Was it His own people who were hypocrites? I fell to my knees and I asked God to extend to these people mercy and grace and not judgment. I pleaded with Him and I asked Him to forgive them for they know not what they do. I cried and cried until I finally fell asleep. In my sleep, I had another dream.

In this dream, Jesus and I were walking arm in arm. I had on my armor and we both had swords in our hands. As we were walking, I noticed that Jesus would pull out His sword and use it. I was puzzled because I could not see who or what He was fighting. However, I realized that He was fighting the spirit world who were coming against me, my enemy and His. As we continued to walk arm in arm, one of my friends joined us. In any event, as she began to speak, Jesus pulled out His sword and attacked her. I looked at him as if to say, "What are you doing? Lord, why are you fighting my friend?" He looked back at me and it was as if I read his thoughts. Suddenly, I heard His thoughts say, "Ann, she is not your friend." I was baffled! I could not make sense of what He said without speaking! My heart began to pound and I could not process what He was doing. As we continued to walk together, arm in arm, I looked at Him and reminded Him that He has given me His Word, His Authority, and His Name. I also reminded Jesus that I could fight my battles because He has equipped me with what I need to fight on my own. However, in this dream, let me reiterate, it was as if He talked to me without saying one word and yet

◄ TOUCH NOT MY ANOINTED

I understood what He was saying? He looked at me and His thoughts told me to trust Him and do not try to understand any of it. However, what I did not understand was why He would use His swords not only on the invisible, but also the visible, who I thought were my friends. As we continued to walk together, arm in arm, we were approached by people over and over again, and Jesus looked at me and again, I read His thoughts. He asked me, "Are you going to fight?" I looked at Him and I could not understand why I needed to fight my friends. I was torn with two impulses—the urge to explain to God that I did not want to fight my friends or just trust God, so I did the latter. I then pulled out my swords and we fought the people together. When I awakened the next morning, I was puzzled and I did not understand the dream. I had questions. I sensed that my God was trying to tell me in my dream that the people who I thought were my friends were indeed my enemies, or was He trying to warn me of the danger of trusting everyone? Again, I was torn between two impulses—the urge to forget about this dream and not to think about it again or I could see this dream as being a message, an alarm or a warning. After I had this dream, I could not think of anything else. I meditated on this dream for days and weeks and all of a sudden words from the Bible flooded my heart.

Exodus 14:14 The LORD will fight for you; you ...—Bible Hub

Verse 14.—Ye shall hold **your** peace. "Do nothing, remain at rest." **Do not be afraid** of them; the LORD **your** God himself **will fight** for you." ... 2 Chronicles 20:17—,29 You shall not need to **fight** in this **battle**: set yourselves, stand ...

I came to a conclusion that I had some enemies who I thought were my friends and in this dream I believe that He was preparing me for difficult times ahead. However, He wanted me to know that He had my back!

I realized the people whom I choose to be my friends hold the key to my future. I have to be very selective in choosing my friends wisely. I pondered this in my heart until I believe I received another word from the Lord. **"The righteous shall choose their friends carefully. For the way of the wicked will lead them astray" Proverb 12:26 –(NKJV).**

He reminded me of the dream that I had concerning the baby I had in my hand, running from the wolves and these wolves represented hypocrites. I believe that He was saying to me that He had chosen me to be a mouthpiece for His kingdom and the call that He has on my life could be blocked, hindered or held back if I chose the wrong friends or the wrong people to hang out with. I believe that there are people who the devil puts in your life to hinder your efforts and to block your progress. The enemy will use anyone to try to stop God's purpose and plan to be fulfilled in your life. On the other hand, I believe that God will bring into your life divine appointments and strategic alliances to line up the right people to help put in place the call that He has on your life. However, I also believe that the enemy will line up the wrong people to try to stop God's plan in your life from being fulfilled. In any case, I have come to believe that if you have a call on your life, the wrong people will sometimes be drawn to you and it will be up to you to love them at a distance. Do not get me wrong, I am not saying that all people who God does not want in your life are bad people. Some of these people can be good people with pure motives, but for some reason God will remove them from your life for a season. I realize that some things I will not understand until I get to Heaven. However, I will always try to trust God in what He is doing in my life and I will always try to obey Him. You see, when you have an anointing on your life, you have to protect it. The anointing is not something that you should take lightly. There is a price to pay for the anointing; and the price is not cheap. If you want the anointing on your life, it is not always going to be ice cream and cake; but sometimes you are going to experience some bitter along with the sweet.

OPPOSITION

I have to warn you, when God has anointed you and you begin to step out, or if you are called to do anything great in your life, you will run into opposition and you begin to make people mad. However, I am reminded of the verse Proverb 19:21—"Man makes plans but only God's plans succeed."

In any event, you have to then realize that you are fighting something bigger than yourself. One morning when I was meditating on the Word, this word came to me in my heart.

"Ann, my beloved child, all of your life you will be a much loved child by your father in heaven and the enemy will be after you but I have overcome the world." So far my dad has been 100% on target but I am not afraid, for God is with me.

There are evil forces in this world trying to keep you from your destiny! I realized through my experience, when you are going somewhere in life, you will face opposition. That is a "no brainer." In *John 16:33 it states—(NIV), "I have told you these things, so that in me you may have peace. In this world you will have trouble. But take heart! I have overcome this world."*

Let's look at an example in the Bible: the Book of

◄ TOUCH NOT MY ANOINTED

Nehemiah. You all know the story. I am going to paraphrase it to make a long story short.

Nehemiah was a cupbearer to a Persian king. During the course of time, Nehemiah found out the walls in Jerusalem were broken down and He asked the King if he could take some time off to go and build up the walls. The King agreed and Nehemiah and some workers went to Jerusalem to restore the walls. However, it was not easy. There were two men named Sanballat and Tobiah who were influential local politicians. When they found out that the building of the walls was going well, they were absolutely furious. They did everything they knew to do to stop it, but God's plan prevailed and the walls were completed in 52 days.

Sometimes the things that you do for God will not be popular nor appreciated by man; and sometimes you may be judged and criticized by some people, thus shutting you out of some circles, but that is ok because you are in God's circle and that is all that really counts. Nevertheless, if you continue to stand your ground and trust in God, no matter what comes against you, God's plan for you will always succeed!! Ask Nehemiah!

I remember one pastor once said that being anointed by Heaven's perspective is not always going to be pleasant in ours. That is definitely an accurate statement.

I would like to give you another example of a person who was anointed, yet He experienced many obstacles, trials,

OPPOSITION

tribulation, pain, hardship and difficulty, just to name a few. Can you guess who this person is, it was Jesus Himself. He was misunderstood, abandoned, rejected and betrayed and miserably mistreated. When He was here 2000 years ago, He sailed against the wind, He swam against the current and He went against the odds. He knew how to protect His anointing. He did not fight every battle. He did not argue every case. He did not try to prove to people that He was right. He did not try to play up to people to win over His critics and above all, He was never drawn in against evil that came against Him. He ignored them and like Pastor Joel Osteen said, "He paid them no mind." He ignored their insults and comments and slander and He did not give them His attention. Jesus did not waste any time trying to make people like Him, for He was not a people pleaser but He wanted only to please God and that is exactly what He did. He just focused on His purpose and ran His race and finished the course and did everything that He was called to do. He is the perfect example to follow. We have to remember, no matter what you go through, you have to focus on God and be obedient to Him and Him alone. He did not let people squeeze Him into their mold, and He did not bow down to their pressure because it definitely takes away favor from God and it takes away your power. Like I said before, if you do anything great in life, you will always come against opposition. Evil forces are always lurking around the bend. It goes without saying, you will always have critics. Not everybody will like you, but that is ok. Everybody did not like Jesus. If everybody does not like you, rejoice, because you are in good company!!! I would say that I have always been in that company.

It began even when I was small and even when I was not saved. As a child, I was different and I am still different now. I believe that one of the reasons I was and am different is because God has showed me so many things, and He gives me so many dreams and visions. Often, He also speaks to me in His words. I have seen angels in my dreams and I have seen angels in real life. I have seen lids on jars that I could not open and after I prayed, I have seen the lids turn and pop right open before my eyes. I have seen things beyond my understanding and supernatural occurrences that defy logic. God is real to me; He is more real than this world. If you would have seen what Jesus has shown me, you would be different too. How can I be normal when God has allowed me to step out of the natural and into the supernatural and He allowed me to step out of ordinary into the extraordinary? Yes, I would say that I am different. Most of my life, I have been rejected and abandoned and underestimated, misunderstood and even betrayed. I have been looked down on because my thinking is different. At one point it used to bother me when I saw things differently from a lot of people, but now, I embrace my difference. Why? Because I believe that God made and continues to be making me this way, different. Years ago, one of my friends sent me a thank you card and on this card, she said that I was like Joshua and Caleb, because they had a different spirit from the rest (Numbers 14:24, NIV). If you get a chance, read about them in the Bible.

OPPOSITION

Often, I pause for a moment to consider my life and the conclusion that I often come to is how I am so blessed to know that God loves me just the way I am. He tells me that I am chosen and that I am anointed and I am appointed for just a time as this. I listen to Him and I take heed and most of all I believe Him. Before I met the Lord, I wore labels on me that said that I am a failure, an outcast, not usable and do not measure up. However, I do not wear these labels any longer because I wear God's Labels. I believe that His labels say that I am a new breed for the 21st Century and I am His masterpiece!!! He said that I am a pearl of a great price and a hidden treasure! He also said that I am blessed, deeply loved, and highly favored by Him and that I was and am a rare breed. I believed that He went on to say that He will give me treasures of darkness and riches in secret places. In any case, I have new labels and these labels give me my new identity! I remember as if it was yesterday, one time as I was on my knees praying to Him and I was distressed and discouraged and my heart was heavy.

I heard a voice within me say that I was His daughter and nobody messes with me!

How awesome is that to know that God is your Father and He has your back!!

One day when I was praying again, I believe that God spoke this word over me.

"Ann, I take great delight in you and I will always quiet

you with my love and I will always rejoice over you with singing!!"

As I listened to these words within me, my heart was pounding and I could not comprehend nor process the depth and the height of how much He loves me. I could not make sense of all this. I thought to myself, how could someone like Him, the maker of this whole Universe, love someone like me? I fell to my knees and tears began to flow without ceasing. As I was crying and my heart was pounding, I believe that His word came to me once again. These words were tender and passionate and heart felt. These words fed my spirit as if it was food. I chewed on them and swallowed them and digested them and I could not stop weeping. It was almost like this love was more than I could stand.

"Ann, nobody messes with you and gets away with it!

You are mine!! The love that I have for Israel, my first born,

Is the same love that I have for you!!"

Suddenly, I realized that this is the second time that He spoke this over me. I remember long ago, someone said that when He repeats Himself, God is saying that this is very important to Him. I know that all of His children are important to Him but when He reiterates it over and over again how much He loves you, you will be compelled more than ever to really believe Him!

OPPOSITION ➤

When He spoke these words to me, I was torn between two impulses—

The urge to repent for hidden sins—sins that I did not know about and sins that I even thought about and yet, I thought about His grace and how much He has already forgiven me. Suddenly, I felt His presence abiding in my apartment and it felt like an Oasis of Heaven. I stood up on my feet, I felt charged, refreshed and renewed in the spirit. I knew I had an encounter with my Father who art in Heaven!! I had an encounter with The Holy One of Heaven who was determined to convince me how much He loves me. The Father of Abraham, Isaac and Jacob, The lover of my soul.

This was not a dream, it was real!! Instantly, I was led to open the Bible and I turned to this page in the Bible. I had it already highlighted. It was as if God had another message for me. It was God continuing to speak to me in His Word.

But Jesus said to them, "A prophet is not without honor except in his own country among his relatives and in his own house." Now He could do no mighty works there, except that He laid His hands on a few sick people and healed them" Mark 6:4-5 (NIV).

When He led me to this verse, I asked Him if this was a verse for me and He was quiet and said nothing!! Day after day, I meditated on this verse and I could not think of anything else. It was almost impossible for me to sleep. My

◀ TOUCH NOT MY ANOINTED

spirit was grieved!! My heart was heavy and I could not process any of it. There is a message in that verse and I am not sure what the message is. I am almost afraid to hear what this message may mean and again I was torn. I do not ever want to be in the dark and yet, I am afraid to know what God is saying to me through this word. Whatever it may mean, I will obey my God. I say to Him at this very moment-

Lord, speak to my heart and reveal to me the truth of this dream that I spoke about in the last chapter and the truth of your Word.

I then asked God not to let me stay in the dark forever and do not stay far from me for trouble is upon me and no one can help me but you!

Meanwhile, after I prayed this prayer, the mystery was later revealed!

This verse came to me:

In the Book of Matthew 13:53-54 (NIV) **A Prophet without Honor**

[53] When Jesus had finished these parables, he moved on from there. [54] Coming to his hometown, he began teaching the people in their synagogue, and they were amazed. "Where did this man get this wisdom and these miraculous powers?" they asked. [55] "Isn't this the carpenter's son? Isn't

OPPOSITION

his mother's name Mary, and aren't his brothers James, Joseph, Simon and Judas?

Suddenly I believed I received a word in my heart and it was

"Their view of you determined their level to receive from you."

Suddenly without warning, situation after situations occurred, (not one or two but many, almost weekly, at church) and then it hit me like a thunder bolt all at once and my eyes came open and it brought me back to what I believed God was saying to me and then I knew clearly the interpretation of the dream of the pack of wolves that tried to stop my voice and that Scripture in Mark 6:4-5:

But Jesus said to them, "A Prophet is not without honor except in his own country among his relatives and in his own house." Now He could do no mighty works there, except that He laid His hands on a few sick people and healed them." Mark 6:4-5

I have realized one thing and that is—A dream or a word from God can sometimes define who you are and will give you a new perspective on things! I will not be limited on how other people define me and they define me by what they see; and I will not live up to other people's low expectation of who they think I am!

I remember pondering that in my heart and crying on my pillow for days, even weeks and feeling deeply hurt and all alone. Nevertheless, I also felt a resolve in my spirit. I then knew why I was left out in prophetic prayer meetings at the church I was attending! As I looked back, in the beginning, I was invited to these prophetic prayer meetings, but then all of a sudden, I was not invited anymore. Why? Because I was not timid in voicing my opinion when I knew I was hearing from God. However, most of the time, my opinion was different from the rest. Although on some occasions if my opinion was different, I would bow down to their pressure and begin agreeing with them. This is wrong and I made many mistakes. I have now learned that if I believe God is speaking to my heart, I should take a stand and not give in to peer pressure.

I have learned that hindsight is 20/20. When I believe God is telling me something and one of my peers or even a leader is trying to change my opinion, I will say, "I mean no disrespect and I hear what you are saying, but that is not what I believe God is telling me about this situation!"

I learned the hard way, like Pastor Jessie Brown said, "If you build your life on your knees you can stand for anything!" It does not matter what anybody else thinks" Romans 3:4 (NKJV) states, "Let God be true but every man a liar."

For example, if you are a part of a group and you do not act like them or speak like them, or even think like the group, you will be rejected; and on numerous occasions, I

OPPOSITION

was rejected and alienated! Why—because my beliefs and opinions were quite different from the rest of the prophetic intercessors group and eventually I was not invited to their prophetic prayer meetings anymore!

As I think back, one day I was walking in the corridor at church, a lady whom I had never seen before, (quite frankly, I have never seen her again), walked up to me and touched me and with a stern look on her face, she said, **"Prophets are not without honor except in their own town."** At that time I had no idea what she was talking about so I smiled and walked away and without a beat, she seemed to disappear! However, it was not until much later I realized she confirmed to me the same verse that I believe God spoke to me. **Please read that verse!** (Mark 6: 4-5)

I have learned from prior experience that when God speaks to me in His Word, He almost always confirms His Word by speaking it again a second time through one of His prophets or an angel or just a friend, even if the friend is not saved. Let me reiterate, I was getting confirmation after confirmation. Yes, God can use anyone! In the Bible, He even used a donkey! Numbers 22:28 (NIV).

In the meantime, I prayed for the church prophetic leaders and the prophetic Intercessors at the church. I prayed that God would open their eyes (prophetic leaders) and cause them to see how they are behaving and remind them that although I was different I am His child too. Sometimes I believe that some people can be sooo religious that they miss out on the revelation of what is right in front of them. I did not realize it back then but I realize it now that the environment was too small for my gift to be realized. When you are in a limited environment with limited thinking, it can make you have a limited life. I knew down in my spirit God wanted me to leave the church but I kept making up excuses not to leave.

That day, I also prayed that God would send me my husband to help me to continue to hear from Him and know what to do concerning this situation. I drank from His (God's) fountain and drew from His well and I stayed on my knees and fasted from eating all day and eventually my heart was at peace and in the process of time, a word came to me in my heart and I believe that I heard from God. Although it was a heart breaking revelation, I received it. I went to my desk and I wrote down what I believed He was saying to me.

"Anyone who tries to belittle or disregard the call that God has on your life is not your friend. Their view of you will determine their level to receive from you! It's time for you to make a transition, Ann, it's time for you to move. The brook is dried up here."

I believe that God sent me my answer and almost at the same time, I believe that He also sent my husband. I paused to carefully consider what I believed I heard from God and I was torn between two responses. I was so happy that God sent me my husband; on the other hand, I would miss my friends. But I knew I had to obey my father.

OPPOSITION

I am sorry that I cannot go into details about other situations that occurred at the church, because I still love these people. Looking back, I am reminded of the saying, "Do the right thing when the wrong things are done to you!"

As a matter of fact, I had second thoughts about mentioning this, but I believe in my heart that there is a will for my life and this book, greater than my fear of what some people may think or do! I am here to please my father not man. Moreover, I believe that certain situations must be told because sometimes something must be done. I also believe that God redeems our story to help other people to realize that they are not alone!

He alone examines *the motives of our heart.*

If this happened to me, I am quite sure that it has happened to others at this church. God is a righteous God and He hates injustice. Again, I am reminded of His word. "When the world around you says be silent, God says: "I'm going to give you a voice." As you see, that is what my God is doing! He is giving me a voice!

In Isaiah 60:15, it says—New International Version "Although you have been forsaken and hated, with no one traveling through, I will make you the everlasting pride and the joy of all generations.

Listen to me, Beloved. I have a question for you? Whose child are you? Better yet, who is your Father? If you do not

◄ TOUCH NOT MY ANOINTED

know who you are, you will be bound by what people think. I know who my Father is; do you? If you do, don't just know Him, believe what He says about you.

I have since left the church—I believe at my Father's leading. I also believe with all of my heart that the hand of God is directing my steps. I have gotten married to a man after God's own heart and we have purchased a home that my husband and I adore and I believe that we have found the church of God's choice. We are still praying about it at this point.

We are so blessed and I could not be happier! God has given me the desires of my heart. I prayed for a nice home and a man who loves God more than I do. I also prayed for a man who has a head for investments. Larry, my husband, loves God with all of his heart and he has a head for good investments. It is almost like God groomed us for one another. My dreams are coming to pass and his dreams are also! Thank you, Lord, for complete healing, restoration and a new beginning.

I give God all the honor and all the Glory!

Recently, I woke up from sleep in our new home and my heart was so happy and I believe that I heard my heart say, "Well done my sweet child, well done! You have only just begun to live and now where you have walked, you will begin to run. "When you run after what is in front of you, you will escape what is behind you!" Your gifting will now begin to be enhanced by me!"

OPPOSITION

Instantly I began to cry because I know just how much my God loves me and this is just the beginning of a new life! Oh, how God loves me and now I can be who God says I am!!

This reminds me of Abraham when he parted from Lot and God began to speak to Abraham. It was not until Lot left that God brought Abraham into his fullness! When you get a chance read about God telling Abraham to leave his family and leave his country but Lot tagged along with Abraham. Later on Abraham told Lot to separate from him (Genesis 12:1-5).

God Promises Canaan to Abraham

Lot has the choice land, but Abraham has God's promise:

"The Lord said to Abram after Lot had parted from him, 'Lift up your eyes from where you are and look north and south, east and west. All the land that you see I will give to you and your offspring forever. I will make your offspring like the dust of the earth, so that if anyone could count the dust, then your offspring could be counted. Go, walk through the length and breadth of the land, for I am giving it to you'" (Genesis 13:14-17).

I believe that God is also calling me to separate from people who would minimize my life.

I would like to share with you what happened immediately

after I left the church and took a vacation as a result (I believe) of my obedience to God! First of all, I went to a prophetic conference while I was on vacation and this is what happened! I wrote this on Facebook!

April 7, 2014

Hello my Beloved! I am still on vacation and I love it soo very much!

Recently, I heard about "A Prophet Conference" and I believed I was led by God to go and I went. While I was there I heard words that I believe were out of the mouth of God Himself! I was blown away with what they had to say to me personally. These prophets took time to speak a word of knowledge to each of us. I had three of these prophets to speak into my life. I went and sat in the midst of them and one of the prophets started to sing, "Oh how He loves you" and then he gazed at me and asked me if I knew how much God loves me and I said, "Yes, I know." Then staring in my eyes with love and intensity, he began to speak again as if he was recalling a distant memory. He asked me for a second and a third time, if I knew how much God loves me and I once again said yes. He paused for a moment and began to carefully consider what he was about to say. He said, "You are like a Mary (the mother of Jesus) to God and He loves you soo much! You are favored among women! He went on to say, even when you were small, the Lord wanted to speak through you, but people stopped your voice and even now, people, even in leadership have

OPPOSITION

tried to close your mouth, but God protects you because He loves you!"

Suddenly, another prophet spoke. He said "Do you know that you have always been misunderstood by many? I believe God is saying to you today, that He does not misunderstand you!! He loves you and you are favored like Mary in the Bible!" And then it hit me like a tidal wave that three different prophets compared me to Mary in the Bible! I was speechless!!! I wanted to speak, but I could not!!!

Oh how I wanted to cry. The tears did not come, although I wanted them to!! My heart was pounding and my hand began to shake and I knew that Almighty God was speaking directly to me through these prophets and also through the movie. Some of these prophets were students who graduated that same night from "The school of prophets!" These student prophets are the ones that spoke in my life! I could go on and on but I have already said too much! My life has been changed because I finally got confirmation of what I already knew! Now I understand why God wanted me to go see the one night showing of the movie—"Mary of Nazareth!" and this "Prophet Conference!" Wow!!!! Like Mary, when she went to visit Elizabeth, who was also pregnant, celebrated her pregnancy; not only did Elizabeth celebrate her, but also appreciated who God called her to be! (See below) I too felt appreciated that day when I went to "the Prophet Conference." Thank you, Jesus!! This was a gift to me from God, a gift unspeakable for words!

55

Let me back track a little bit. Before I went to the Prophetic Conference, I believed that I was led by God to go see a one—time showing of Mary of Nazareth at the Celebration Cinema in Lansing. In the movie, the angel Of God Gabriel came to Mary and told her that she was favored among women and that the Holy Spirit was going to come upon her and impregnate her with a child and as Gabriel was talking to Mary, I felt that God was also talking to me. My spirit was leaping and I could not sit still. I paused to carefully consider the implications of what my Father was saying to me. He was talking to Mary but I also believed that He was talking to me! He then told Mary that her cousin, Elizabeth, was also pregnant with child which also would be a miracle pregnancy. Mary told her family and her fiancé and they could not comprehend or compute in their heads what Mary told them so she traveled to see her cousin, Elizabeth. When she arrived at her house, Elizabeth was pregnant just like the angel had said. Better yet, when Elizabeth saw Mary, she just knew without anybody saying a word that Mary was also pregnant! It was a confirmation of what the angel had told her. That day Mary felt understood and appreciated regarding who God called her to be! Meanwhile after I went to see the movie and my fiancé and I traveled to Pennsylvania to the Prophets Conference and when they spoke with me, they seemed to just know my whole life story and they also knew the plans that God had for me! That day, like Mary, I too felt appreciated of whom God called me to be. That word came at a critical time for me!

OPPOSITION

I remember very clearly as if it happened yesterday! Immediately after this conference, my whole life changed! I am still amazed how God my father knew that I needed to hear these prophetic words spoken over me. All three of these prophets were totally used by God Himself! I remember going into my hotel that day and looking up Luke 1:28. It said "O favored one (endured with grace)! The Lord is with you!" I remember looking up favor and it said, favor-empowered to prosper, supernatural have an advantage for success—empowered to accomplish everything I have been called to do because I have God's favor at work! I realized that day that God strategically orchestrated my steps from the day I stepped down from my job at church until now! Yes, He is still speaking and I am listening and waiting! I know that it will take time to prepare and grow more deeply into the person He has called me to be but at least I know now that I am on the right track. I ask this question again. Whose child am I? Often I feel like I am a throwback from years past like Joseph in the Bible. My life sometimes seems almost unreal. I appear to be more like my descendants, Abraham, Isaac and Jacob than the Christian people of this world. Yes, I am a child of God. He is my Father!

I know that I was and am called by God to be one Of His servants, yes, even His prophet! I know that this may sound spooky to you but God is more real to me than this world! This next chapter you will see how God does not only warn me about groups at a church but He also warns me about the wrong friends—

A SECRET BETWEEN YOU AND ME

Sometimes God even forewarns me in advance about things and other times He allows me to go through things because I know that I am never alone. He is always with me. If I did not know that back then, I know that now.

I would like to tell you a secret, only between you and me. This is not about a church but it is about people in general! When someone (a person) comes into my life and God does not approve of them being with me, He lets me know it. Whether it is in a dream or a vision. I have to admit something that I am not too proud of. When I was a child my mom said that I was sooo naïve and too innocent beyond words. Unfortunately, I believe that I still am today and as a result of me being so naive, I believe that God protects me and warns me of trouble ahead!

If I can, I would like to share a dream that I had concerning a person who I thought was my friend. I had this dream years ago and in this dream, this person was sitting on the couch in my living room. However, this person was not a person, it was a monkey. I was talking to this monkey as if it was a person. Suddenly, I awakened from this brief dream and within hours of me leaving my apartment I went to this store and I saw my friend and all of a sudden, I looked at her and I saw her face as a monkey. I was in shock. I could not process what I thought I was seeing. In any event, she came up to me in this store and she hugged me and she had a face of a monkey. When she hugged me, I almost had an urge to run! I could not think straight and my heart was heavy. I knew it was her in my dream. I came home and looked up the word monkey in the dictionary, Webster and dictionary.com and it said—

Monkey—fool/joker/to mimic/ to mock—

A person who causes trouble.

After I read the meaning, I just did not want to believe that she was the monkey in the dream. I did not understand what God was trying to say to me so I would still talk to her when I saw her and we still went shopping together. We would sometimes talk for hours on the phone. In any event, I had a second dream similar to the first one. It was a body of a lady and a face of a monkey. This person was also at my house in this dream. This time I took the dream seriously because since it was given to me a second time, I knew this was very important to Him for me to act on the message that He was giving me. Slowly, and cautiously and carefully, I knelt down on my knees and I asked God to reveal to me who this person is and what did He want me to do about her? Later in the week, I saw her again and I again saw a vision of her having a monkey face. However, I continued to speak to her sometimes but then, one day, someone told me that this person and one of her friends would talk about me behind my back and mock the way I talk. She told me that this person would always make fun of my voice and laugh. I was so hurt but I should not have been surprised. One day she called me on the phone and she actually confirmed what this other person told me. I remember as if it was yesterday that she said to me, with a trace of amusement in her voice, that her and her friend (fiancé) laugh at the way I talk. I asked her why and she said that I talk like a cartoon character. She laughed at me over the phone and did not think one thought about it. I did not feel any anger, but I felt sadness. I thought she was my friend. I paused to carefully consider how someone could claim to be my friend yet make fun of me behind my back. Unfortunately not too much later, she and her fiancé broke off their engagement and I never knew why. I was deeply saddened by the split up because I knew how much she loved him.

I remember asking God to help her and to bring her closer to Him. I prayed to God for Him to give her an encounter that she will never forget. I also prayed that God would take her by her hand and tell her how much He loved her. I went on to pray that God would bless her exceedingly and abundantly above all that she could ask or think. Lastly, I prayed that blessings would chase her down like wild horses and come upon her and overtake her. As time went on, I gradually separated myself from her and I never had a dream like that again.

I was deeply hurt but I guess I was forewarned. I really loved her and I really miss her even now, but separating from her was not only a good decision—it was the best decision I have ever made. I thank God every day for causing me to walk in the light, and not in darkness. He is and always will be my best friend and my protector. I know now that she was never my friend. A friend is not a person that talks about you and laughs at you behind your back. If that is a friend, I do not ever want any. Whenever someone talks behind your back in a mocking way, always remember that everything is naked and open to the eyes of the Lord. He sees everything!! He says, "Vengeance is mine said the Lord, I will repay." When God gives you a dream and you know deep down inside that it is from Him, pray about it and if He tells you to do something, do not take it lightly—otherwise it could be some serious ramifications. Moreover, If He gives you the same dream or speaks to you twice about the same thing, always remember that whatever He is saying, He is very, very serious and He wants you to take precautions. Proverbs 27:12 says:

Parallel **Verses** ... A **prudent person** foresees danger and **takes precautions**. The **simpleton** goes blindly on and **suffers** the **consequences**. English Standard Version The prudent **sees** danger and hides himself, **but** the simple **go** on and **suffer** for it.

As a side note, I would like to say that anytime God speaks to you about anything, be obedient to Him and obey quickly, whether it is the first time or the second. In this case, I believed that God spoke to me in this dream but I was not sure what He was telling me to do so I just

TOUCH NOT MY ANOINTED

prayed about it until I was certain I heard from God as to what He wanted me to do!

Always remember to trust God because He always has your best interest at heart. God loves you with an everlasting love and He will never lead you astray.

When you have a call on your life, the enemy will try to use anyone he can to get you off track. He will try to use people to cause you to walk in unforgiveness, bitterness and pride, but if you walk in God's unconditional love, the enemy will not be able to touch you.

DRIVEN BY LOVE

It is the love that holds the key to your future.

In any event, whenever I have a dream and God repeats this dream over and over again, I know that God is speaking to me loud and clear. He wants you to be wise and not a simpleton. This bears repeating and every time I think of it, I should mention it! "Be wise and not a simpleton!"

I also know that He is telling me that whatever the message He is trying to convey to me, He is serious!!! My father is always driven by love.

Moreover, I do know one thing and that is if I continue to walk in love and forgiveness, His plan for me will ultimately succeed. I believe that God is preparing me for greater things like He did with Joseph, no matter who tries to stop me. I will always walk in love no matter what.

When you walk in love, it is the highest form of spiritual warfare against the enemy. The enemy will not block you or stop you or hinder you or hold you back. Why? Because you always walk in love, no matter what.

When God gives me a dream like the one I just spoke about which I at first do not understand I keep asking for an interpretation. He sometimes repeats the dream over again, or He sets a note in my path so I can read it and He answers me with the note. It is almost like I had written these notes before, because it is my handwriting, but He transports them from one place to where I can see them and read them. This sounds strange, but it sometimes happens this way. You have to remember that God can do anything. He can even write like me, and maybe sometimes it is His handwriting not mine. What an awesome thought and an awesome God!! Everything He does and everything He says is driven by love. Why? Because God is love!

You have to remember that great events in the Scriptures are hinged on dreams. Joseph was told in a dream that one day his brothers would bow down to him. When he told his brothers about this dream, it made his brothers angry at him and they were determined to get rid of him (Read about Joseph in Genesis 37).

However, God was preparing Joseph for greater things.

When I think of the dream of Joseph's brothers bowing down to him, I am reminded of the verse in Proverbs 14:19—(NIV).

"Evil men will bow down to the good and wicked men will stand at the gates of the righteous."

If you read about Joseph, you will see that Joseph had some jealous and evil brothers and in Joseph's later years, his brothers did bow down to him in Genesis 42. If you would ask, how was Joseph able to persevere in time of trouble?

Answer—I Corinthians 13-(NIV) covers that completely! Joseph walked in love!

"Love is patient, love is kind, love is not rude and love is not easily angered. Love is not boastful nor proud nor self-seeking. Love does not count wrong done to it. Love never fails."

Pharaoh also had a dream that showed him the future. God also spoke to Nebuchadnezzar in a dream in much the same way as He had spoken to me.

Now I see why God wanted me to write this book, so I could see what he has been trying to show me all of these years. It is so clear to me now. As I write this book, my life is unfolding before my very eyes.

<u>I would like to once again repeat what I said earlier. The devil may succeed in delay but he cannot succeed in denying what God has for you as long as you walk in obedience and also walk in love. Always remember that Love is the key to your future!</u>

I feel like a complete idiot. God's message whether it is in a dream or a vision or a prophetic word, has been so loud and clear!! However, my defense is as fragile as a clay pot.

◄ TOUCH NOT MY ANOINTED

I have a question for myself.

Who have I been listening to? Beloved, hear me, no matter what people may say to you, it will not stop God's destiny for you!

How could I not know all these many years what God has been so clearly trying to say to me? Although, I was not totally in the dark, I was not fully persuaded either. But I am now, fully persuaded!! I will only listen to my God and His voice alone will I follow! (John 10:1-21) I will never again dismiss the gift that I believe God has given me, but the gift means nothing, if I do not walk in love. This gift of prophecy was customized by God for me and me alone. I will be like an eagle, bold, confident and full of faith— strong, powerful and authoritative. No longer will I be timid, shy or fearful, but I will also be like a dove—meek, kind and gentle. If the crows try to crow at me and chickens try to peck me or the hawk tries to bait me into battle, I will fly higher and like my favorite, Pastor Joel Osteen, said, "Pay them no mind."

I would like to pray to God this very moment.

"God, forgive me for being so hard of hearing. I hear with my ears but sometimes I don't really listen. Teach me how to hear your voice, never missing a word that you say. I am not blind but sometimes I do not see and I am not deaf but sometimes I do not hear.

Lord, forgive me for being hard-headed. But even now, I know that you are my papa and you love me and you forgive me.

"God, speak to my heart clearly and tell me what to do and where to go. I do not know where to begin. Papa, continue to give me wisdom and revelation and sharp discernment, Lord. I cannot do this without your help. Even now I know that your love is like a fire that lights my way. Father, when I go astray, send a light and send the truth to lead me back to you. Papa, also send me divine connections and strategic alliances that will help me on this journey. Send me, Lord, someone who loves you (even more than I do). Lord, I know that I am as an Eagle, but Lord, no matter how high I fly, I will still need you!! In Jesus' name, I pray.

After I prayed this prayer, I believe that God put me to sleep and I had another dream that I was climbing a mountain and it looked like I was climbing it alone. However, on the way up this mountain, I began to stumble and someone from the back rescued me. As I continued to climb the mountain, I looked back again and I saw many people walking behind me. I believe the Lord was trying to tell me that I was not going on the Journey alone and that He had sent me what I asked for!! He is sending me help and I will be leading the way as long as I follow Him. What a beautiful awesome God!!! I have realized that our journey consists of passion and struggles, difficulty, hardship and pain and also beliefs that are painted by our Father.

◀ TOUCH NOT MY ANOINTED

Suddenly, I got on my knees and praised Him with all of my heart and without a beat. I believed that I actually felt His presence, which is His love!

One day as I was reading His Word, I once again felt a need to praise Him! This prayer is my friend, Barbara's, prayer that she likes to pray.

I said, "God, if there are no figs on the tree, no grapes on the vines, no cattle in the stall, no food in the fridge and no money in the bank, yet I will forever praise you and I will always be driven by your divine Love!"

I remember when I was a child, my mom would always say to me that I had such an innocence because I took what everybody said to me at face-value. I thought everyone told the truth. Even when I dreamed, I believed it.

A CHILD OF DREAMS

I would like to share with you my life as a child and how God, even back then, would speak to me and I believed that my mom knew in her heart that God had a huge call on my life. However, I believe that it scared her!!

Even when I was a little girl, I would have these dreams and real visions and they would all come to pass. I remember sometimes when I would have these dreams, I woke up from my sleep and my heart was pounding and I could not think straight and I could not process the thoughts. They would be prophetic dreams. The dreams were like a mystery or a message or even a warning alarm.

These dreams would seem so real, as if they were actually happening right at that moment. Sometimes when I had visions, it felt as if I was in a trance for a second and then my sight would come back to normal. I believed my dreams because most of them seemed to come true.

I believe if Mom had listened to my dreams and taken hold of them, our lives would have been dramatically influenced by them.

At some point, my mom did not want to hear any more of my dreams because I believe they frightened her and I never really talked to her about my visions. I figured that if

she was not sure about my dreams, the visions would have really troubled her so I never told her about them. Though the visions that occurred were sporadic, the dreams that I had were almost every night or every other night.

Let me share one of my dreams with you. I was a little girl probably around four years old and I had a dream that we (our family) were standing outside and I did not see our home, but I did see trees down on the ground pulled up at the roots as if a storm had totally destroyed everything in its path. I remember thinking in this dream, "Where is our home and why does there seem to be so much confusion, chaos, and disorder"? I was not sure what this dream meant at the time. I knew something was about to happen; however, I had no idea what was coming. I had no idea what was about to happen or what it was all leading up to; but I knew something was going to happen. I simply did not know what or when it would occur.

I shared it with my mom and she said that it was just a nightmare. She asked me not to share any more of my eerie dreams with her or with anyone else because it brings on panic, anxiety and dread. She said that was not what people need to hear so I did not press the issue.

My mom always wanted to hear pleasant things; and if I told her something to cause panic, anxiety or dread, she would refuse to consider the issue or avoid addressing it. My mom was a mom of peace and love. She hated anything that was the opposite of peace. I loved my mom and

A CHILD OF DREAMS

I always respected her and obeyed her because I knew just how much she loved her kids, including me.

However, weeks later after my dream a tornado came, the thing that I predicted!

This was not a dream, this was real!!

During that time, my dad was in the army. Needless to say, it was just my mom and my sisters and brothers. The storm was so bad that Mom asked us to go outside in the storm. I did not understand that; but as we left our home and ran outside, we saw a huge funnel cloud in the sky that passed over our neighbor's house and came down and totally destroyed our home. Although I had a dream about this very thing, it still did not seem real!

It was like a nightmare except it was real and it did not go away.

At one point, I remember closing my eyes and when I opened them, my brother, Harvey, and my sister, Linda, were barricaded under all the rubble. My mom was screaming for help but there was no help in sight. I was the youngest at that time so my mom had me cradled in her arms holding me so tight that I could hardly breathe.

All of a sudden, I noticed that my mom was talking. I looked up at her and she was talking to someone who was not there, someone who was invisible. I know now, but I did

◄ TOUCH NOT MY ANOINTED

not know back then, that it was God who she was talking to.

She was crying and talking at the same time. I believe that this was the first time that I ever saw her praying, and I was so amazed that He answered her prayer, not right away; but soon.

Suddenly, our neighbor (who lived a couple of houses from us) I believe his name was Joe Frank Massey, appeared in our presence as if he was an angel and he lifted the rubble and the uprooted trees and the debris from my brother and my sister. They were bruised and in shock but they appeared ok and they did not need to go to the hospital (at least, that is what my mom thought). My mom put me down and grabbed both of them in her arms and she couldn't stop crying. She was hugging them so tight, she did not want to let them go. I remember at one point she set my brother and sister down on the ground beside her and she fell to her knees and lifted both of her hands in the air, thanking someone and crying.

She was crying and thanking Him at the same time. I had no idea at the time what she was doing, although I knew whoever she was talking to was not seen but he seemed powerful!

I KNOW NOW IT WAS GOD WHO SHE WAS PRAYING TO, IT WAS GOD WHO PROTECTECD US!

A CHILD OF DREAMS

Our family hardly ever went to church. We would sometimes go on special occasions but even then I do not remember Mom ever going to church. (However she did have an intimate, passionate relationship with God. I found this out much later).

Getting back to the turmoil. I could see in my mom's face that she did not know what do. She was troubled. She was in a dilemma. Her heart was troubled like a wild sea in a raging storm. Keep in mind that Dad was off to war and Mom was in charge of all of us kids and it was five of us and seeing how the tornado destroyed our home we were left homeless and we had no place to stay. Our house was totally demolished. As Mom looked around, there was destruction, ruin, and spoils everywhere. Trees were pulled up from their roots and the cars were tossed over like toy cars in the parking lot. Our family lost everything. As I remember looking around, I saw the walking wounded. People's faces were damaged and their bodies bruised. Stuff was flying in the air; and children were carried miles away from their homes. Houses, including ours, uprooted and totally demolished! At one point, I saw a child in a tree nearby as if she had climbed the tree herself! She looked as if she was almost hypnotized and yet she was not crying but more or less in shock of what happened!

A while back, I went to see the movie "Twister." It really brought back memories, even though I was a small child. I will never forget it! It will be forever seared in my memory.

◄ TOUCH NOT MY ANOINTED

As I think back, it was as if this violent tornado had a mind of its own and it was driven by an evil spirit that was determined to destroy our family. My mom (whom I believed had a word of knowledge from God, coupled with remembering my dream) led us quickly out of our home and I was in her arms. Immediately, I turned and looked at this wicked funnel cloud and it passed quickly over our next door neighbor's home and suddenly it swept down and totally destroyed our home. There was nothing left standing. I was so numb and all I could do was stare at all of the damage and confusion around us. There were piles of rubble all around us! The whole thing just did not seem real but yet I saw this devastation in my dream weeks back.

What I do not understand is why the funnel cloud passed over our next door neighbor's home and it came with a vengeance to our home. It was as if this storm had an agenda and it was us. Although this tornado was devastating, I remember looking at this violent funnel cloud and being sooo amazed how it seemed to know exactly where it was heading and why it was going there! It was if it had a guided missile focus and nothing was going to distract it or get in its way!

Our home was totally demolished! Nothing, absolutely nothing, of our home was left standing!

However, I believe if Mom would have listened to me and made preparation for this storm in advance, maybe somehow we could have saved our home. Then again, maybe not. The fact that all of us was saved was nothing short of a miracle!

In any event, because of Mom's quick decision (as a result of the Word that I believed she received from the Lord to get out of the house) we were all saved. We had two people in our family get hurt but we all survived. May I repeat, it was nothing short of a miracle!

I do not remember how long that we were homeless. It could have been a day or maybe just several hours, but we had to stay with our Aunt Freda who was one of my mom's older sisters. She was married and had one daughter. They lived in a two bedroom apartment. It was so small and we were so crowded! It was Mom and five of us children in this tiny apartment along with my aunt and uncle and their daughter. It was nine of us, altogether, living under the same roof and it was not a house; it was a very small apartment!

But we did not complain because at least we had a place to stay. Even back then I believed that God protected us.

I remember one night when my mom and I were in the living room of my aunt's house, I asked Mom about the dream that I had prior to the tornado and she stared at me without saying one word. It was a look I would never forget!!! If looks could kill, I probably would be dead. However, eventually she looked directly at me and she spoke with a tone intense and slightly sarcastic and her voice was somewhat filled with tension. I am sorry, I do not remember what she said but I do remember how it made me feel when she said it! (I almost felt sorry that I even had that dream!)

(Just a note. I do not want you to think that Mom was mean because she was not. She was the best mom anybody could ever have! She loved her family and God was always first in her life!) In my opinion, she was almost close to perfect and had a perfect heart toward God!

Nevertheless, I knew right away that in this dream I was given a glimpse of what was soon to happen yet no one really cared.

Isaiah 42:9 New King James Version (NKJV)
[9] Behold, the former things have come to pass,
And new things I declare;
Before they spring forth I tell you of them."

I did not understand it all at the time, because I did not know the Lord and I did not know His Word, but I believe that He knew me and my mom. I also believe that God had chosen me even as a child to be separated from the world and consecrated unto Him. He chose to give me dreams and visions that I did not understand, but I would ponder them in my heart and meditate on them day after day. This may sound strange, but I believe that there was a slight possibility the enemy was in the tornado and that his focus was not to kill my family but I believe that he was after me,

A CHILD OF DREAMS

(God's Anointed). He knew even before I did that I was set apart and that I was going to be God's Anointed. Better yet, it was if I was already anointed, but I did not know it because I did not know God!

Sometime after this tornado happened, I began to pray to God, but I did not know Him. I only knew of Him. I prayed to Him every night because I wanted to be like my mom. After the storm, I would notice my mom praying all the time and when she needed help, she always managed to get it. As a side note, I imagine mom prayed all the time even before the storm, but I did not realize it.

In any event, it seemed like we stayed at my mom's sister's house a long time. But our dad finally came home from the army and we moved into our own home. It was so good to be in our own home. My father had our home built just for us. We all felt blessed and favored and deeply loved.

After the tornado I was not allowed to share my dreams, or should I say nightmares, with anyone. From that time forward, every dream that I had, I pondered in my heart. I would pause for a second to figure out the significance of it. I knew even then that my dreams were different, but I also knew that they were very relevant and far-reaching. It was as if the Lord was showing me the future before it happened. I knew in my heart that these were not ordinary dreams. There was a purpose and plan, even warnings in some of these dreams of things to come. I did not quite know back then, but I know now, that these dreams were prophetic. Even as a child I was unaware of what was happening but I believe God was preparing me for His purpose, and He was going to someday use me to be a catalyst for change.

On rare occasions, my mom allowed me to share some dreams with her. I believe mother understood that some of my dreams were meant for her to pray over. However if the dream was not too strange, she would allow me to share it with others. At that time, I did not understand why my mom did not want me to share all of my dreams with the family. Nevertheless, I now have a better understanding of what my mom was doing. I believe that she was trying to protect me from being misunderstood. As you read the book of Genesis, Joseph's dreams turned his brothers against him. I believe that my mom was trying to prevent this from happening to me. At least I believe that was one of the reasons.

Now that I know the Lord, I have so many questions. Look at Moses. The Pharaoh tried to kill him when he was a baby because of his anointing. It did not work because God protected him (Hebrews 11:23-NIV). It was by faith that Moses' parents hid him for three months when he was born. They saw that God had given them an unusual child, and they were not afraid to disobey the king's command.

When he grew up, it was him (with God's anointing) who freed his people. Exodus 3:7 New King James Version (NKJV)

7 And the LORD said: "I have surely seen the oppression of my people who *are* in Egypt, and have heard their cry because of their taskmasters, for I know their sorrows.

Moses was the Israelites' Liberator. He freed the slaves. God anointed Moses for this task!!!! Look at Jesus' life when he was a child. His life was also in jeopardy. Why? Because He was a chosen vessel also used by God to free His people. In America George Washington led the original fight for independence. A century later Abraham Lincoln set three million people free. It makes me wonder all the more if the enemy tried to take their lives when they were children. I do not know if George Washington and Abraham Lincoln were even saved; but I do know that God used them in a powerful way and they seemed to love God and loved our nation.

You are probably wondering where I am going with this. Well, I am kind of wondering the same thing. At any rate, I believe God is using me to write this book. However, I believe my writing is just the beginning of something much more to come.

This bears repeating. I believe that the enemy wanted to take me out when I was small because apparently, there is a huge call on my life. I believe that God was preparing me when I was small for a greater purpose. When I was a little girl, my family would watch some movies on television and we would see these beautiful angels. I remember asking Mom if they were real. However, I do not remember her response. In any event, I would imagine angels following me wherever I went and I actually felt protected. I said that to say this: maybe the enemy did actually see angels around me and that is the reason he was trying to take me out. I believe he was trying to kill me before I came into my calling. Apparently, he was really threatened by the call that was upon my life.

I sense right at this very moment that my future is going to be in a totally different place than where I am today and I will not be restricted by my past. I believe that the veil that was over my eyes is beginning to be lifted and I will not have any limitation or even care about what people think. My concern is what God is calling me to do.

In any event, I believe that as God protected Moses and Jesus, He also protects me. I am not trying to compare myself to Jesus nor Moses; I am simply trying to get a point across. Somehow the enemy knew that God was going to use me big time when I was fully prepared so he tried to stop me when I was young. He saw that God was using me even before I knew him so I believe he wanted to close my mouth to stop me from speaking God's Word through my dreams.

I remember I dreamed of alligators in our home, specifically under one of my sister's bed. This dream really frightened me, but I did not tell anyone; I just pondered it in my heart. I would carefully consider in my heart every dream that I believed was from Him.

A CHILD OF DREAMS ➤

Immediately after I had this dream, my sister became very ill. It was under her bed where I had seen these alligators. The doctors did not know what the sickness was and why it came about. I know now that alligators in a biblical sense represent evil. Even today she is still having some problems.

Again, although I was not allowed to share most my dreams (after the tornado) I knew that someone was speaking loud and clear. I did not know who nor why they chose me to speak to, but every day I pondered those dreams in my heart, knowing that they would someday come to pass and they always did. Every time I dreamed, I always paused to carefully consider what each dream may mean. I believe God was speaking but no one seemed to want to hear Him but me!

Since no one wanted to hear what I believe God was speaking in my dreams, His message did not go forth. Like I said before, I believe that Mom wanted to protect me from being misunderstood by the family, so, therefore, she did not want to hear my dreams. However, Satan used that to try to stop God's progress and, unfortunately, he did. I used to sometimes wonder why I was given these visions and dreams, since I could not share them. I would say to myself if someone was trying to give me a message and I was not allowed to share it, what purpose would the dream serve? I used to sometimes wish that I did not have this gift because it was almost like an illusion and yet it was always a foreshadowing of something bigger coming, and something

TOUCH NOT MY ANOINTED

always came. Whether it was storms, difficulty, hardship or trials or tribulations, I believe the dreams had purpose and meaning. When these dreams manifested themselves, it would be like a (dream) drama replaying itself in real life.

THE STRANGE ONE

Mom always treated me the same as my sisters, although I was different. In school I was a loner and I did not have many friends. However, most of the teachers took to me because they said that I had a knack of always telling the truth. When a teacher left the room and there were disagreements or fights between students while the teacher was out of the room, my teachers would look to me to tell them the truth as to what really happened while she (teacher) was away. This was because I always tried to tell the truth. I must admit, it got me in some trouble with the rest of the students.

My sister, Linda, was a year older than I but she was physically stronger. Whenever I had arguments with anyone, she would just appear and come to my rescue and all the people my age were afraid of her. She was like a tomboy and she could really fight. No boy or girl her age or older could hold a candle to her strength. It was as if she had a rage inside of her when she became angry and no one could stop her. When she was angry, she was like a tornado! I would say that she was unstoppable.

However, she was the sweetest sister. She was so quiet, timid and very kindhearted. She never had much to say to anyone, but when she talked, people would listen, like what they used to say about E.F. Hutton (smile). But

◄ TOUCH NOT MY ANOINTED

if someone made her angry, she would pick up anything that was in her way and would throw it. You could almost compare her to the show "Incredible Hulk," where he was a normal man but when he was upset he would turn into the Hulk, a creature of enormous strength. Sometimes, if you made Linda mad, it was as if she turned into a different person, a person that I did not know! She was my sister, but I never really understood her. She was always a mystery to me. However, to my family, I was more different than her. They could relate to her, but not to me. I was, in my family's opinion, "the strange one."

In any event, I always wanted to be physically strong like Linda and be able to fight but I was just the opposite. If a feather flew by me, I would be frightened. I remember asking Mom why my sister, Linda, could fight so well and I could not fight at all. It used to bother me but Mom assured me that we all are different and each of us are gifted in different ways. I remember asking Mom, was it a gift to have a temper and she said no, but it can be a gift to be strong, if you channel that gift to something productive. Like Samson in the Bible, God gave him strength and I believe God also gave Linda strength. In any event, I was very glad that she was my sister. No one would bother me and get away with it because if someone was picking on me, Linda would always just appear out of the blue and defend me. I believe that God sent Linda instead of sending His angel. I remember coming to the conclusion when I was a little girl that Linda was my angel and being physically strong was definitely her gift and, boy, did I appreciate it!

THE STRANGE ONE

On the other hand, speaking of gifts, I believe that one of my gifts is prophecy. Sometimes I understand them (dreams) and sometimes I do not. Whether I was small or an adult, almost ninety percent of my dreams would come to pass and that would sometimes frighten me. Seeing how I could not share most of my dreams when I was small, I would write them down and watch them come to pass. Again, I say that my dreams were not only a mystery but also a message, I believe, from God. Unfortunately, no one knew except for me and God, although at the time it was kind of a mystery in my mind who God was. Let me reiterate, I knew of Him, but I did not know Him.

I did not understand who was talking to me in my dreams nor why I was the one chosen to see the future.

I did not know what it all meant and I did not know how to interpret it. As I said earlier, not only did I have dreams but I also had visions. I would like to share a real vision that I had when I was small and it was prophetic. If I remember correctly, it was as if I was daydreaming and my daydreaming turned into a real live vision as if I was in a trance.

In this vision, a lady was sitting next to dad in the front seat of our car and I was curious as to what this meant.

I remember seeing my dad in his car with a lady and I was appalled by this vision. I did not know who she was. I thought about this vision for days, and for days I could not think of anything else. I did not share this vision with anyone for I knew if I did, I would have gotten myself into trouble. One day as I was lying on my bed, I paused for a moment to consider what this vision meant. In any case, my silence was so intense, I was afraid of what that vision might mean. I was torn with two impulses—the urge to forget all about the vision or to investigate it.

In any event, I decided to investigate it. I was in elementary school at the time—I believe I was about 12 or 13 years of age. The next day, after school, I decided to walk by my father's work-place to see if he could give me a ride home. He got off from work about the same time that I got off from school and his job was not that far from school. As I arrived at the location of my father's job, (I believe that he worked at the Lincoln County Hospital at the time) he was getting into his car. I saw a lady sitting in the front passenger seat. My heart was pounding and I could not think straight—I could not process what my eyes were seeing.

I ran to the car and I looked at my father and I said with a voice tense with anxiety. "Dad, who is this lady and why is she sitting in the front seat of your car?" At first the silence was so intense, I was afraid of what he was about to say. It was like my vision replaying itself in a real life modern day drama. He then looked at me and he reluctantly spoke with a voice filled with tension. He said that she worked with him and he was just giving her a ride home. He asked me why I stopped by today, seeing how I never did it before. I paused for a moment gazing into my dad's face, making no attempt to hide my disapproval. I looked at him and spoke in a tone that was slightly sarcastic. I told him that I would tell him later about the vision that I had. (I could sometimes tell dad my dreams and visions without him becoming angry with me.)

In any case, I wanted to see if this vision was prophetic and it was. It happened just like I saw it in my vision and it happened the very next day! Immediately, the lady looked at my dad and politely asked him if she could get out of the car. However, he did not respond to her question. Instead, he looked at me and told me to get in and he started up the car. In any case, as we were driving home, the silence was so intense I could almost hear my own thoughts. Just before we arrived home, he let her off. She thanked him and she walked the rest of the way home. Her home was very close to where we lived. As my dad and I were driving home, my dad looked at me and said (his voice tense with anxiety), "Honey, do not mention this to your mom, because you know how she is. She would not understand." As I gazed at him, again I made no attempt to hide my skepticism. But I reluctantly agreed that I would not mention it to Mom. However, I asked my dad to do me a huge favor. He said "anything" and my tone was intense and slightly sarcastic. I asked him not to ever give her or any other woman a ride again in our family car because it doesn't look right. He reached over and kissed me on my forehead and he said that I was quite different than the rest of the family and he asked me if I knew that, and I said nothing.

However, my dad went on to say that I was a rose among

thorns. He said that I did not seem to have a temper like the rest of my siblings unless someone had really provoked me. He reassured me that it was a good thing. He also said that it did not take much to set off the rest of my siblings. "But with you," he said, "it normally takes a lot to make you angry." In any case, he looked at me with a slight smile and he said that he admired the love and devotion that I had for our family and he again reassured me that he himself had that same commitment to our family.

I paused for a moment and carefully considered every word that he spoke. I slowly, carefully and cautiously reexamined every word.

Again, I gazed at him and I asked the same question. I was not impressed with his first response. I was persistent. I wanted my dad to realize that giving a lady a ride home in our family car was not acceptable and if anyone saw him with her they would possibly draw the wrong conclusion.

However, I knew that my dad was trying very hard to avoid the question, so therefore, I paused for a moment to consider if there could be a message behind this vision. However, my dad reassured me that this was a one-time occurrence and he would not give any lady a ride in our car again unless it was an extreme emergency. In any event, after the initial shock wore off and the trauma lessened, I looked at him and smiled. I believed that he told me the truth. I looked at him with a demeanor and tone less guarded and

I told him that he was the best dad in this whole world. In any case, he paused for a moment and he looked as if he was carefully considering what he was about to say. He once again looked over at me and said that I was a rare gem, different from all the rest.

I was quite amused and intrigued at my dad's words, but all I could do was smile.

I do not want to leave you in suspense concerning this lady and dad. If you knew my dad, you would know that sometimes my dad could be quite complicated. He was almost like a paradox. In other words, he could be the sweetest person anyone could ever know and he could break your heart with his kindness. On the other hand, he could be as distant as the stars. Nevertheless, if anyone needed help and he was there to help them, he would be the first person to lend a hand. Moreover, if this lady did not have a ride home, he would feel like it was his responsibility to help her. I believed that it was an innocent one-time occasion and that it never happened again, although I could be wrong. I can only hope.

I did not know back then why I would get all this information (vision) and where it came from. The vision of this lady in my dad's car actually did happen. Now I know that these dreams and even visions were given to me by God. They were preparing me for such a time as this. I am not sure why God allowed me to experience these things at such a young age, but there is and was a reason greater than anyone can even think or imagine. The bottom line is "I trust God."

You are probably wondering whether or not I ever mentioned this to my mother. I never did. I promised my dad that I would not mention it to her, and I try to never break a promise. I am a person of integrity (at least I always try to be). Besides, daddy was right, Mom would not have understood! Take my word for it!

As you have noticed, I have always had this gift as far back as I can remember. There have been times that I asked myself if these dreams were actually a gift or a hindrance. Nevertheless, I have to believe that I was conceived for the purpose of the will of God and I have to believe these dreams are a gift from Him. Like Moses, and Jesus and Esther and yes, Joseph, many people in the Bible were separated from this world and consecrated unto God to fulfill the purpose and the plan that He had for their lives. I, too, feel chosen! I hope I do not sound arrogant or proud or boastful, but these are facts. Not only I was different as a child, I was very unusual and I still am!

On the other hand, somehow being different or being unusual does not seem to fit with proud or boastful, but rather it seems, according to the world's standard, to go with the word "misfit." But my Father in Heaven calls a misfit "A Pearl of a Great Price."

I just went on my merry way, wondering if there were more

kids like me. I knew that I was different, but I believed that I was different in a good way, at least that is what my dad said, my earthly dad.

GOD HEALS

I remember in the second grade I became very ill. I missed almost a year of school. Because of that I was held back one full year. The doctors did not know what was wrong with me. I could not breathe very well. It was like I was starving for air. I had a tightness in my chest. My bronchial tubes were swollen and became plugged up with mucus. I would not be hungry so therefore I would not eat. I was so skinny and my mom was not only concerned about my health but she was also concerned about my weight. I was nothing but skin and bones!

My mom and dad would try to force feed me so I would not die of starvation. No matter what they did, it would not work. I did not have an appetite and I did not want to eat anything. All I could focus on was this terrible sickness. There were times that I wanted to die. I felt that I had no good reason to live.

I had terrible headaches that would almost never let up. I had some kind of cough but I did not have a cold. I remember going through this torture weeks and months at a time with no relief. The doctors did not do any lab work or test of any kind. My dad did not understand why. My father kept taking me to different doctors in Tennessee, even beyond my home town. However no one seemed to know what to do. I was not diagnosed. I went through this for a long time—at least for a year or so. These were some of the darkest moments of my life. My dad and I would sometimes sit in silence since he had no words to make me feel better. (He was the quiet, moody type.) I was so sick, my dad thought that I was going to die. He stayed up with me almost every night trying to help me, even though he had to be at work at 5:00 a.m. the next morning. I would often see him lying by my bed crying for hours until it was time for him to get ready for work. More times than I can remember, my dad and I would be lying on my bed, crying together. I was crying because I was in so much pain and I just wanted to die. However, my dad was crying because he hated to see me in pain. He did not know what to do so he helped me cry. My mother and father loved me so much and they wanted so much to spare me from this pain.

One day my father and I were sitting on the bed and I looked at him and said, "Dad, thank you." He looked at me with tears in his eyes and he said, "For what?" and I said, "Thank you for sharing in my suffering." He looked at me and said nothing; but his tears spoke volumes.

My dad was a man of few words, but when he spoke, it came directly from his heart. We were always so close. I felt like I was his favorite. Perhaps it was because I suffered so much and he knew that I needed him.

As a Christian, you, too, can be on call as a willing vessel to opportunities for intentional sharing through your presence when someone is suffering from an illness. You can make a huge difference, even if you are not sure what to say or how to say it. No one should have to suffer alone, whether they be your family or your friends. My dad was always there for me. My dad was my dad and he was also my best friend.

One day he decided to take me to a doctor out of state. We lived in Fayetteville, Tennessee and he and I traveled alone to Huntsville, Alabama. If I am not mistaken, Alabama is not too far away from where we lived in Fayetteville, Tennessee. We went back and forth to Alabama and the doctors finally did some lab work and eventually we had a diagnosis. The diagnosis was asthma and bronchitis. I remember the doctor stated that asthma can be difficult to diagnose, because its symptoms may resemble those of other diseases, including emphysema and lower respiratory infections. The doctor in Alabama said that because of the diagnosis and appropriate treatment, I was spared from serious danger. However, I know different now. It was because God healed me. It was because God had His hand on me and I did not even know it. I knew someone was watching over me, but I did not know who.

I believe with all of my heart, the enemy continued over and over again to try to take my young life, like he wanted to take the life of Moses and many more in the Bible when they were young also.

Immediately after the diagnosis, the doctor put me on some medication and I started to feel some relief. The more

GOD HEALS

I took the medication, the symptoms gradually let up. From that time on, my life changed and I began to live a relatively normal life. Although sometimes that sickness would try to creep up on me due to stress, lack of sleep, anxiety and strong negative emotions. However, I knew that I was going to be alright. I knew that I had a call on my life and I knew it was going to be fulfilled.

Meanwhile the doctor from Alabama contacted my local doctor in Tennessee with the proper diagnosis and treatment. I no longer had to travel to Alabama to see him. This was a huge relief for me and my father.

During this time my mom was extremely busy taking care of five kids. So my dad was basically my caretaker at home. It seemed like my mom was pregnant most of the time I was sick, and all of her pregnancies were extremely difficult, according to my sister, Freda.

Although my dad worked a full time job, he also worked several side jobs, plus he took care of me full time. I have always understood what it is like to have a great dad. However, I know now that my father in heaven is not just great, He is perfect, and He loves me unconditionally! I am not trying to minimize all the wonderful things my dad did for me on earth. However I do know that my dad's love paled in comparison to my heavenly father's love because He has perfect unconditional love!!! Everything about my Father in Heaven (God) is perfect!!

TOUCH NOT MY ANOINTED

As time passed, when I was about 10 or 11 years old, the doctor did not understand why I no longer had any symptoms of asthma. He said that it was rare that all the symptoms would disappear. He was amazed that I was asthma free. To this very day I've never had any more problem with that sickness. Although I did not realize until years later that it was God who intervened on my behalf and healed me. I give Him all the honor and glory.

PROPHETS

You are probably wondering, where I am going with this. What does this have to do with "the anointing"? Let me give you a recap of what I have already told you.

When I was a child, I believe that God anointed me to be separated from the world and consecrated unto Him. As an adult, I believe that God dropped that in my spirit so I would know that I was one of His chosen. I also believe that the enemy was after me. I believe that this sickness and the destructive tornado were methods that the enemy used to try to destroy my life. It did not matter that I was just a child. He knew that I would be used by God to advance His kingdom. Just like the enemy tried to take my life, He also tried to take the life of many biblical characters when they were children, and many of God's anointed, whether it was in biblical days or the present age.

I would like to talk to you about Moses.

Read the Book of Exodus in the Bible and how God used Moses as His anointed!! Pharaoh was the king of Egypt at this time and at first he welcomed the Hebrew guest to Egypt. As time passed he realized the Hebrews were multiplying and this threatened the security of Egypt. Pharaoh thought that maybe one day, they (Hebrews) would take over and make the Egyptians their slaves. In light of this, Pharaoh ordered the murder of male Israelite babies. However, Moses' parents hid him among the grasses of a swamp. There the baby caught the eye of Pharaoh's daughter. The very thing intended to destroy the Israelites led to their deliverance. Pharaoh's daughter adopted Moses into the palace and paid Moses' mother to nurse him. Though he was the son of a slave, yet he was brought up in power, preparing the way for his destiny. While he was in Egypt, he saw a Hebrew being beaten by an Egyptian and he killed the Egyptian. Moses fled Egypt and stayed in the wilderness. While he was there God revealed himself to Moses in the form of a burning bush. You see how God worked behind the scenes to rescue His anointed and eventually used him to free His (God's) people. I believe the enemy tried to destroy Moses as a child but God always came through with a vengeance. After forty years of being in the desert, God anointed Moses to go back to Egypt to free His people. God also revealed the Ten Commandments to Moses. Moses even spent forty days and forty nights in the presence of God. The very presence of God was Moses' anointing. On his own, Moses could never have dreamed or imagined what God's purpose was for his life. Moses even pointed out his limitations to God. God saw beyond that. Moses was destined for greater things. Remember the anointing is for a time and purpose and a season. The anointing is always from God for a specific purpose. The anointing has nothing to do with your emotions. It is not about you. It's about God working through you.

If you are willing to be a nobody (like Moses and yes, even me) God will anoint you and make you a "some-body."

You see, God had a purpose and a plan for Moses even before he was born. Always remember this, beloved: what God has for you will come to pass! No devil in hell nor physical attack, nor gossip about you will stop God's plan for you. It will come to pass! God always has the final say! We serve a great God and we should have great expectations. If you have asked Jesus into your life, He is actively involved in your life. Do you see Him active or do you see Him passive. Graham Cooke said your image or your picture of God will drive your expectation of who He is and what He can do in your life.

I would also like to give you a modern day example of God's anointing me to speak into a young man's life at my church.

I was a part of the Back Room Intercessors at my church. We interceded for our church service. We had different teams that met on Sundays. I remember every time that it was my scheduled time to intercede, I saw Paul walking back and forth in the hallway. Later I found out that he was part of security. Eventually, I believe that God told me that Paul was a chosen one, the instrument for His purpose, and he was "His" anointed. I guess at first I was baffled. I was unsure of what I was supposed to do or if I was supposed to do anything. Then one day as he was walking in the hallway, he looked at me and I realized that it was

◄ TOUCH NOT MY ANOINTED

time for me to give him a message. I took him aside and began to tell him what I believed God had revealed to me concerning his life. He looked at me and did not seem at all surprised by what I was saying to him. It was as if I had spoken what he already knew. He then told me of strange things that happened to him during his childhood, when he was very small. He went on to tell me that one night while staying with his grandparents, while he was sleeping a car crashed into his bedroom. It was as if something or someone was out to destroy him. From what I understand, if I am not mistaken, this was not a rare occurrence. I am not sure about the details of what happened after the accident but you see there is a real devil in the world and if he could, he would destroy all of "God's anointed" even as children, so that God's purpose and plan will not be realized. In spite of what some people may think, God has anointed this young man for a purpose and a plan and it will be fulfilled! God (Himself) will see to it! I do know that this young man is going to college now. He is a chosen vessel that God is using tremendously. I believe with all of my heart that this young man is an instrument of God's purpose, a new breed.

God is more real than this world and He will protect His anointed because "he who is in you is greater than he who is in the world" 1 John 4:4-(NIV) You, dear children, are from God and have overcome them, because the one who is in you is greater than the one who is in the world.

No weapon formed against us will prosper, it may form,

◄ 100

but it will not prosper. Based on what I read in the Bible and my personal experience, the bottom line is,

If you have a great call on your life, the enemy has assignments on your life. However, if you walk in fear, you definitely do not know who God is and what He can do!

A short time after I spoke to this young man I was approached by his mother. At the time that she and I met, I was able to share with her what God had revealed to me about her son. I mentioned that God was raising up a remnant who will be free from the burden of false pretense, free from the burden of offending the person who is being used by the enemy and free from the burden of being offended. God is raising up a new breed who only listens to Him and not man. God is raising up a new breed who love the Lord first and foremost. The remnants will not see through natural eyes but they will see through the eyes of faith. They will walk in humility, holiness and repentance and they will devote themselves to the secret place.

I shared with her that her son was one of God's remnant who has been called for such a time as this. To my complete surprise, she was in full agreement. It was so refreshing to see that the young man's mother not only had an open mind, but she seemed to take what I said without any reservation. She was so thankful! She even asked me if I could type what I said and give it to him and I agreed. It not only encouraged her but he was encouraged also. He went off to college and I have not had much contact with him since, but I still pray for him as often as I can.

Recently I was reading the Bible and I decided to read Numbers Chapter 13. (Paraphrasing) I remember reading in Numbers that God asked Moses to have spies go into Canaan to check out the land which He had given to the children of Israel. So Moses sent in spies to Canaan and when the spies returned after 40 days, they came back and told Moses that this land flows with milk and honey but the people who dwell in the land are strong, the cities are fortified and very large and the people said that there are giants in the land. They also said that they were not able to fight against them because the people in that land were stronger than they were. However Caleb said, "We could go up and take possession of the land because we are able to overcome it." Nevertheless, the children of Israel gave them a bad report, and they did not want to go. Those men who brought the evil report died by the plague before the Lord. But Joshua and Caleb remained alive because they brought back a good report. Joshua and Caleb believed that if God gave them that land, God would empower them to take it.

Joshua and Caleb had a different spirit than the other spies. They thought differently from the rest and in the end, they were the only two that were allowed to go to the land of milk and honey. There is much to be said about being a remnant and being an Emerging Leader. I said that to say this. I believe that the young man named Paul is like

PROPHETS

Joshua and Caleb. He has a different spirit also, different from most people his age. A different spirit is an indication of anointing.

If I may, I would like to share with you one example of my thinking being different than the rest. I was going to a church in Lansing (Pastor Hogan's church in the year of, I believe, 2000 and I loved the pastor). He is so anointed! He was definitely led by the Lord in everything he did and said. However, I became a part of his women's group and I believed that they did not really reflect who he was. One night at a meeting, we were in a circle discussing God. They all agreed that if you had a small request, you did not need God's input. They believed that you only pray to Him about large requests. They seemed to think that when you ask Him about small things, you are wasting His time. However, I was the only one to disagree. I expressed to the group that I asked God about everything, including the right dress to buy or the right watermelon to select. They seemed to think that was funny. They laughed in my face and they thought that I was cute. On the other hand, I was serious and I wanted to be taken seriously. I felt underestimated and looked down upon and I felt totally misunderstood and disrespected! I felt that I was treated like a child and I was probably way over the age of forty. How would you like being treated like a child in your forties or even fifties? It is not very pleasant. However, to have child-like faith is quite different from actually being treated like one.

This was, however, not a rare occurrence at this particular

church. I hated to leave but I believed that it was time for me to go and I left.

However, my conclusion was that the pastor's leaders in that church did not represent the pastor nor God very well. They represented themselves and themselves only. Sometime later I believe the church closed down! What a tragedy for the awesome pastor! I do not know the details of what actually happened!

After I left and found another church, I continued to pray for the pastor and his congregation. I know in my heart that God will continue to use this powerful man in a miraculous way!

Why? Because I have a picture and an image of who God is and it drives my expectation of what He can do. He can turn around what the enemy meant for bad and turn it around for His good!

I am waiting to hear more about what God is going to do in this pastor's life. God is awesome!!

Before I knew God, I wore labels on me that said that I am a failure, an outcast, not usable—one who does not measure up. However, I do not wear these labels any longer, because I wear God's labels. He says that I am chosen, I am anointed and appointed and restored and valuable and redeemed and victorious. He says that I am His masterpiece!!! One day when I was praying, reflecting on my life, I believe that God spoke a word to me and it went like this.

I was not sure what He was saying and I did not know what this message was leading up too, but I was all ears.

ANN, NOBODY MESSES WITH YOU AND GETS AWAY WITH IT! YOU ARE MINE!! THE LOVE THAT I HAVE FOR MY FIRST BORN IS THE SAME LOVE THAT I HAVE FOR YOU, ANN!

As I got up off of my knees, I went and opened the Bible and I turned to this page in The One Year Bible (NLT) I had it already highlighted. It was as if God was continuing to speak to me in His Word. The Word said:

"I KNOW ALL THE THINGS THAT YOU DO, AND I HAVE OPENED A DOOR FOR YOU THAT NO ONE CAN CLOSE. YOU HAVE LITTLE STRENGTH, YET YOU DID NOT DENY ME. LOOK, I WILL FORCE THOSE WHO BELONG TO SATAN'S SYNAGOGUE, THOSE LIARS WHO SAY THEY ARE JEWS BUT ARE NOT, TO COME AND BOW DOWN AT YOUR FEET. THEY WILL ACKNOWLEDGE THAT YOU ARE THE ONES I LOVE" Rev 3:8-9 (NLT).

Immediately, I knew how much I mean to Him. In actuality, God reminds me of this verse quite often. Again, I am not sure why except I believe that I am so special to Him and I know it deep within me. If you have asked Jesus into your life, beloved, you are special to Him also. I believe God favors those who favor Him and I know that He is and always will be my most favorite person in this whole wide world and I let Him know it all during the day, every day.

As I mentioned before, when someone comes into my life and God does not approve of them being with me, He lets me know it. He always gives me a dream that tells me that this person is off limits to me. I do not believe that this person is bad; I just sometimes think that this person may not fit in with who God called me to be. I can't seem to explain what or why God is so protective of me, but I do not care. I only care that He is protective and I love that about Him.

Everything He does, whether I am experiencing difficulty, hardship or pain, everything He does is because He loves me. Everything He allows to happen in my life is because He is trying to cleanse me and make me more like His son, Jesus!! We all have to go through those difficult seasons and those difficult seasons form the process that takes us to the place where He wants us to be. Someone once told me that the process is not our identity, and I agree. However, the process identifies with whom we are becoming one. Like Graham Cooke said, it is 'the process which makes you rich.' How beautiful is that!!!

The whole Bible tells me how much He loves me and who I am in Him. The Bible tells me if we follow after God wholeheartedly, we will be like Mount Zion, immovable!!

You know what?

I believe it!!

THE VISITOR

Everything Jesus does, He does well. Everything Jesus said, He said well!!

Whether it was 2000 years ago or now. My Jesus has successfully convinced me who I am in Him and who He is in me!

When Jesus came 2000 years ago, He had a job to do for His father and it was well done and His anointing was well protected and He pleased His Father and not His critics. Who were His critics? They were religious people. The Pharisees were bound by religion. They were too restrictive, too orderly, too tight and too legalistic. They were hypocrites. They wore gaunt and hungry looks during a brief fast, they wore Bible verses strapped to their foreheads and left arms. God is not fooled or deceived by appearances. We cannot fake behavior to impress him. The Pharisees' outside appearance did not match the inside reality. God knew the reality of who they were. They were not genuine, or real or sincere, nor authentic but they were fake and phony and Jesus knew it. They could not fool Him. However, seeing how they realized that Jesus saw right through them, they hated Him. I am not trying to compare myself with Jesus, but I can sometimes look at people myself and I can see right through them. I can sometimes tell the real people from the phony ones.

TOUCH NOT MY ANOINTED

I sense sometimes that the phony ones seem to know that I know that they are like Pharisees. On the outside, they are like white washed tombs but on the inside, they are like dead men's bones. I will just call them Pharisees.

In any event, when they (Pharisees) see that God has given me discernment and revelation and knowledge and insight to see who they are, they seem not to like me. Do not get me wrong, I am not saying that all the people that do not like me are hypocrites or Pharisees but some are and I can see right through them. I do not announce it to anyone; I just talk about it to God and I pray for them and pray for me. I ask God if He would help them and heal them and deliver them and extend to them grace and mercy. I always tell God if I am wrong, I ask Him to forgive me and open my eyes to see them the way He sees them.

One time as I was praying and I said, "Father, if you will deliver them (speaking of a particular person) and He responded "what do you mean if I will deliver them" and then He said, "I will do it" and in this particular situation, it was done! One of the people that was not living according to God's will totally changed and I saw a dramatic difference in their life.

God can do anything and nothing is too difficult for Him! When you walk in God's will, He will surround you with favor and when you pray, He will always answer you. Sometimes He may not answer you immediately, but He will always answer you!!

THE VISITOR

I walk in favor and I expect favor to come upon me and chase me down like wild horses and overtake me and it does every day!!! Always remember that you have what you say!!! Mark 11:23 (NIV)<u>New International Version</u> "Truly I tell you, if anyone says to this mountain, 'Go, throw yourself into the sea,' and does not doubt in their heart but believes that what they say will happen, it will be done for them."

We must keep in mind that the favor of Heaven's perspective and the gift of knowledge will not always be pleasant and joyful from our perspective.

In addition to being hated by the Pharisees, even when Jesus was born, Herod tried to take His life.

Everybody knows the story of how baby Jesus was born and how Herod tried to kill Him as a baby. However, that task was not accomplished. He lived among us going around healing, delivering and setting people free from sickness and disease.

Instead of many sacrifices, He eventually made only one and that was Himself. Christ's death freed the inheritance for us.

In any event, Jesus died but He was raised up and now He sits on the right hand of our Father interceding on our behalf. What a beautiful end result!!!! Read the Life of Jesus in the New Testament. Matthew, Mark, Luke and John are four gospels chronicling the life and ministry of Jesus.

TOUCH NOT MY ANOINTED

Doing the right thing sometimes seems more than we can stand, but to Jesus, it was like first nature.

Jesus knew His purpose on earth and nothing got in His way. He fought the good fight, remained faithful, finished his course and He received His prize!!!

As I mentioned earlier, He is now sitting on the right hand of the Father interceding on our behalf. Praise be the Lord!!

I believe that faith is what releases the anointing on earth from heaven. When you pour oil on a person, anointing them, it is not the oil that anoints but it is the act of faith that releases the anointing. In spite of what Jesus went through on earth, He never went through it alone. He always went to that secret place and drank from the fountain and drew from the deep well and His spirit was refreshed and it was His faith in God that released the anointing.

I have learned through my experience, you cannot keep giving out and ministering to others without going to your father God and getting refilled and replenished.

How can you minister from an empty well? You cannot.

You have to continue to protect the anointing by going to God and letting Him teach you how to release those hidden hurts such as unforgiveness, bitterness, arrogance, pride and rejection.

Rejection is not only a strong emotion but it sends a toxic message. Rejection says "You do not belong here, you are not good enough, and you do not fit."

However when you go to that secret place and draw from God's well and drink from His fountain, He will tell you that you are good enough and you do belong here and you do fit.

He will begin to teach you how to release those hidden hurts and let go of those past rejections. Then He will draw you to Himself and speak tenderly to your heart and in this place, you will experience a love that is beyond your imagination. Suddenly, you will come into your vineyard of fruitfulness, and in this place you will lay hold of the finished work of Jesus Christ and you will become fearless in the face of difficulty, hardship pain and rejection. Only then will you be able to launch out on your mission one step at a time and have passion for the purpose and the plans of God. How do I know? Because I have been there in that place of rejection and I know what it feels like to be set free! What a glorious feeling!

Two thousand years ago, when Jesus was here on earth, after teaching and preaching, He would always slip away from the crowd and go to that secret place and spend quality time with God. And in this place he would be refilled and replenished.

If Jesus had to slip away from the crowd in order for Him

to be refilled and replenished, we need to do that also. We need to live by His example. What better example is there?

THAT SECRET PLACE

I would like to share an experience with you that impacted my life years ago. At one point in my life, I would go to my secret place and talk to my Lord sometimes three or four times a day and even throughout the day. I would talk to Him about what was troubling me and I would drink from the fountain and draw from His well. This is called "fellowship" or "relationship" and it was very intimate. I would come to Him and share my most intimate feelings with Him and I would pour out my heart on my knees and I knew that I had His undivided attention. In my distress I cried out to the Lord—yes, I prayed to my God for help. He heard me from His sanctuary; and my cry reached His ears. Then the earth quaked and trembled. The foundations of the mountains shook; they quaked because of His anger. He heard my plea for justice and declared me innocent and He rescued me.

As I proceeded to speak, I felt His presence and we were as one. We were in one accord in unity and in harmony. All of a sudden I felt an urge to stop speaking and I began to listen. Throughout my quiet time with Him, on one occasion, I believe that He said to me:

"My love for you, Ann, is strong and passionate and I am consumed with passion for you and you are mine." Then I thought I heard a voice say,

"ANN, I AM HERE, AND YOU WILL MAKE IT THROUGH."

I then saw a vision and it was as if I saw smoke poured from His nostrils; fierce flames leaped from His mouth and glowing coals blazed forth from Him and He opened the heavens and came down. Dark clouds were beneath His feet, and mounted on a mighty angelic being, He flew soaring on wings of the wind. He shrouded Himself in darkness, veiling His approach with dark rain clouds. The Lord thundered from heaven; the voice of the most high resounded and He shot His arrows and scattered my enemies.

As tears ran down my face and love flowed from my heart, I realized there were no words in the English language that would scratch the surface of what I was feeling for Him. I know that the love that He has for me was not because of my performance nor my deeds, but it was because of who He is and what His son Jesus did on the cross. God is love!!! Not only is He love but He is my protector and He fights all of my battles and He always wins!! Better yet, the battle has already been won!

As I continued to listen, I wrote down the comforting words that I believe that He was speaking to me and I not only had the opportunity to release those hidden hurts that were built up inside of me but He also taught me how to let go of those feelings of rejection.

As I let go of those things inside of me, He began to fill me up with His words, His purpose and His plan. At one point, I used to do this every day and when I left His presence I was refilled in all areas where I was empty. In other words, I drank from His fountain and drew from His well and when I came to Him empty, He would fill me up with His love and purpose and truth. When He spoke, I listened and I did not take lightly what I believed He had said to me. I saw myself as a "Mary" who sat at the feet of Jesus taking in everything He had to say. In Luke chapter 10:38-42 (NKJV) it says that Jesus went to visit Martha and her sister, Mary (who sat at the feet of Jesus to listen to His word). But Martha was upset because, instead of helping her prepare the meals, Mary was sitting at Jesus' feet taking in every word that Jesus was saying. Finally Martha stepped in, interrupting them.

"Lord, do you not care that my sister has left me to serve alone? Therefore, tell her to help me." And Jesus answered and said to her, "Martha, Martha, you are worried and troubled about many things But one thing is needed and Mary has chosen that good part, which will not be taken away from her."

Likeminded, I remember being the same way, sitting at the feet of Jesus, taking in every single word He would say to me.

I was lost in the love of my God! My focus was Him and Him alone.

Nothing, I mean absolutely nothing could distract me from

hearing what He was saying to me. I was all ears. I had ears to hear and eyes to see and a heart to obey and I listened and I understood well. Everything I needed was at my fingertips and I was taking in His knowledge and I understood every word; and when I left from His presence, I would make it a point to apply all the information that I was drinking from His deep well. When He spoke to me, His truth was not hidden, but it was clear and simple.

As He spoke, His truth bypassed the head and it went directly to my heart and my heart changed.

In the Bible, Jesus sometimes spoke parables, but with me, He was direct, clear, accurate and to the point; and what He had to say was always free from confusion. As He continued to speak, I would wait quietly before Him, for my victory comes from Him. He alone is my rock and my salvation, and fortress where I would never be shaken.

As time went on, I became an intercessor at church and people would tell me to pray for them in my personal quiet time and I always said yes. I proceeded to do this and at one point, I began to go to God in my quiet time and all I had was prayer requests. I was seeking His hand and not His heart. This went on for months until one day I was praying for the list of names that I had in front of me and after I finished praying, I said "Thank you, Lord, for answering my prayers and I said "Amen." As I began to rise up from prayer, I had a strong thought that came from my spirit and this thought could not have been mine. It was a thought that I could not shake and it hit me suddenly, like a tidal wave! It would not go away. Though I was finished with the prayer, God was not finished with me. Unlike the time before when we used to fellowship, I would talk and He would listen and He would talk and I would listen.

Unfortunately, our relationship had changed, and it was not Him that changed, it was me.

However, I was not aware of it until I had a thought in my spirit and I heard it once again very clearly.

"Ann, where are we?"

When I heard these words a second time in my heart, I knew that God was serious. My heart began to pound and I could not think straight and I could not process what I thought I heard. At any rate, I slowly, cautiously and carefully deliberated every word that I heard Him say.

It was as if I actually saw a vision of Him crying and saying to me,

"I want more than your prayer requests, I want you. I want your heart. I want you to know me."

He went on to say, Ann, I remember a time when you were so eager to please me as a young bride pleases her husband. I hurt and I mourn and I am overcome with grief. I weep day and night longing for you to come back

to me. Ann, where are we"? Come back to me and I will take great delight in you and I will quiet you with my love and I will rejoice over you with singing."

As I began to listen to that still small voice, I believe that I heard,

"Do not just come to me with your prayer requests, I want to feel that you love me."

As His words rang in my ear, and His message burned in my heart, I could not help but cry. I cried until I could cry no more and I fell to my knees and asked Him to forgive me. I realized my listening to Him holds the key to my future.

I then asked myself questions, what good is it to do God's work but to not know Him?" What good is it to do God's work if you do not love Him? If you use the gift that He has given you and you do not have a relationship with Him, that gift is a filthy piece of rags.

Father, I cried, "if I have found favor in your sight and if it seems like the right thing to do, I ask Father that you grant me this one wish and it is for you to forgive me for seeking your hand and not your heart. I prayed, God, My Father forgive me!

O Lord, you are exalted as head above everything else and I love you more than life itself. Oh Lord, I prayed, what are human beings and what am I that you should notice me, a mere mortal that you should think about me? For I am like a breath of air; a puff of smoke, a mist. My days are like a passing shadow, here today and gone tomorrow, gone without a trace.

Who are you? You are God and God almighty and God alone. There is no one like you and no one can be even compared to you. No one, absolutely no one, can measure your greatness. You are my anchor, you are my advocate and you are my God.

I thank you and praise your name. Lord, who am I that you are so good to me? O Lord God of Abraham, Isaac and Jacob. My God, when doubts filled my mind, your comfort gave me renewed hope and strength. When people failed me, your presence sustained me and your love supported me. What would I do without you? I would not even want to live if I did not have you. Who would protect me if I did not have you? Who would stand up for me against evildoers? No one but you. Lord, search me and know my heart, try me and know my thoughts and if there is anything evil hidden inside me, lead me to the way everlasting. Create in me a clean heart, oh God. Renew a loyal spirit within me. Do not banish me from your presence, and do not take your Holy Spirit from me. Restore to me the joy of my salvation and make me willing to obey you. Then I will teach your ways to rebels and they will return to you. Unseal my lips, O Lord, that my mouth may praise you forever. O God, I prayed, my heart is fixed, settled, es-

tablished and fully persuaded that whatever you say, you will do. I believe you. I believe your Word. I will sing and give praise, even with my glory. I will praise thee O Lord among the people and I will sing praises to you among the nations. Be thou exalted, God above the heavens and thy truth reaches unto the clouds. My hope is in you, my confidence is in you, my assurance is in you and my trust is in you and you alone. I ask, Father, that you forgive me for what I have done to you.

I prayed this prayer and my eyes and my heart were filled with tears. I could not stop crying and suddenly, I felt a peace in my room that was unimaginable! God's presence was like nothing I had ever felt before. It was like an oasis of heaven itself!!

I realized that God not only heard my prayer but He answered me and He once again filled my heart with joy and my life with hope. All of a sudden, I found a pen and a paper and I was listening and I believed that He was talking and I wrote what I believed He was saying to me.

My father went on to say, "Ann, I have heard your prayer and I will turn your weeping into dancing, and I will exchange your sadness for gladness. Do not weep any longer for I love you deeply. I love you as I love my first born, Israel. I will show mercy to anyone I choose, and I will show compassion to anyone I choose and I choose to show mercy and compassion to you, my precious Ann."

"I, the Lord, have spoken."

I responded "Thank you, Jesus, Thank you, Lord, for my weeping has turned into dancing!!! Freedom has come and your love has found a way to my heart. Lord, I stand in awe of you and under grace and mercy, you have covered my failings again washing away all of my sins. I will always trust in you and wait for you and always follow you. Teach me, God, how to hear your voice, never drawing back and never missing a word you say. I will always wait for you and trust in you. Never drawing back but giving you everything!! I stand, Lord, in awe of you.

Lord, even if I pray to you and you choose not to answer my prayer right away, I will wait for you and I will always trust in you, because I love you.

Lord, I continued to pray—Lord, please forgive me for seeking your hands and not your heart. I prayed this prayer once again-

Lord, if my fig trees do not blossom and there are no grapes on the vine and the land is empty and barren, I will still praise you, Lord!

Sometimes we get so busy that we neglect the most important thing in life and it is God. We get so caught up in doing God's work and we forget about our relationship with Him and praising Him! If we do His work and we forget about Him, the work we do for Him is null and void. This work becomes a filthy piece of rag (Isaiah 64:6). It becomes our effort (flesh) not God's promises. <u>New Living Translation</u> We are all infected and impure with sin. When we display our righteous deeds, they are nothing but filthy rags. Like autumn leaves, we wither and fall, and our sins sweep us away like the wind.

If you do not have a relationship with Him, what good is the anointing? Sometimes we can be anointed, but not appointed; we do not have the approval of God because we do not have a relationship with Him. We must keep in mind that before we were formed in our mom's womb, He knew us and deposited gifts and talents and potential inside of us. Jeremiah 1:5 says, "Before I formed you in the womb I knew you; before you were born I sanctified you; ordained you a prophet to the nation." However, you have to have a relationship with Him; may I repeat, you have to have a relationship with God. You have to talk to Him, and read His word and allow Him to talk to you. You have to make a concentrated effort to read His word and meditate on it and consume it, devour it, rely on it, lean on it and depend on it and chew on every word like chewing on steak. You have to inhale and exhale His word and digest it. You have to not only know His word but you have to understand it and apply what you have learned every day. Only then can you be anointed with God's approval. How awesome is that!!!! Knowing and obeying God's Word and knowing Him is just a small thing compared to all the benefits that come along with God's promises.

God wants you to know Him because He made you and you are the image of Him. God wants you to want his heart and not just His hand. He wants you to love Him and honor Him and believe Him and reverence Him and praise Him. Why? Because He is God. "Heaven proclaims the glory of God. The skies display His craftsmanship. Day after day they continue to speak; night after night they make Him known. They speak without a sound or word and their voice is never heard, yet His message has gone throughout the earth and their word to all the world. The instructions of the Lord are perfect reviving the soul. The decrees of the Lord are trustworthy, making wise the simple."

God is the maker of the heavens and the earth and He wants you to know and love Him!!

If you get married and you have children, wouldn't you want your children to know you and to love you? Of course you would!!! God is our creator and also He is to some of us "Our Father." He loves all of His creation, though He is not a father to us all. In order for God to be your father, you have to ask Jesus into your life to be your Lord and your savior and you have to mean it in your heart. If you do that, you will be saved and you will not only be God's creation, but you will be His children and He will be your father. As a Father, He will guide you and direct and sustain you. He will watch over you day and night (Proverbs 6:22-NIV). When you sleep, He will watch over you; when you awake, He will speak to you; and when you walk, He will guide you. He will not leave nor forsake you. He will always be your companion. God will be your refuge and strength in time of trouble—always ready to help. So therefore you will not fear when earthquakes come and the mountains crumble into the sea. He merely spoke and the heavens were created. He breathed the word, and all the stars were born. He assigned the sea its boundaries and locked the ocean in vast reservoirs. Let the whole world fear the Lord and let everyone stand in awe of Him. When He spoke the world began and it appeared at His command. The Lord frustrates the plan of your enemies and He thwarts all their schemes, but His plans stand firm forever and His intentions can never be shaken! Read Psalms Chapter 33 (NLT).

If you ask Jesus to come into your life, this great supernatural God will be with you forever. He loves you so much and He wants to feel your love and praise coming back to Him.

How awesome is that!!

Hosea 6:6—(NLT) says, "I want you to show love, not offer sacrifices. I want you to know me more than I want burnt offerings."

When I read that verse, it moves me to tears knowing that He loves us so much and He wants to feel that love and goodness coming back to Him. This bears repeating: you see, if you are anointed and do not have a relationship with Him, and He does not feel your love; it is His gift but it is self-effort which is from the flesh. When the anointing is from the flesh, God does not even acknowledge it. Before I go any further, I am going to pray that as you read my book, it will cultivate a thirst and a hunger and a craving for Him creating a fresh new image and a new perspective, causing you to enlarge your vision and expand your horizon. I also pray that my anointing from God will cause you to worship God with reckless abandonment (lavish praise). If you should ask, what is reckless abandonment? I would say that it is abandoning yourself to the purpose of honoring someone else and in this case, it is honoring and loving our God.

Father, I pray that as the people read this book, that you will ignite in them a fire that will eternally burn in them all the days of their lives a thirst and a hunger for you and for your Word. Father, give them a fresh new vision that will change their image of who you are, drawing them closer and closer to you like never before, causing them to worship you with reckless abandonment, taking them to a level of intimacy that is beyond their wildest imagination, causing them to live in that secret place.

Father, I also pray that in that secret place, they will not just give you their prayer requests, but they will give you their hearts!

In Jesus' name, I pray, Amen"

RECKLESS ABANDONEMENT

I would like to give you some examples of people in the Bible who worshipped God with reckless abandonment.

My first example will be Mary, the Mother of Jesus. I mentioned her early on.

Let's get started! Luke 1:26-38-(NIV)

In the sixth month of Elizabeth's pregnancy, God sent the angel Gabriel to Nazareth, a town in Galilee, 27to a virgin pledged to be married to a man named Joseph, a descendant of David. The virgin's name was Mary. 28The angel went to her and said, "Greetings, you who are highly favored! The Lord is with you." 29Mary was greatly troubled at his words and wondered what kind of greeting this might be. 30But the angel said to her, "Do not be afraid, Mary; you have found favor with God. 31You will conceive and give birth to a son, and you are to call him Jesus. 32He will be great and will be called the Son of the Most High. The Lord God will give him the throne of his father David, 33and he will reign over Jacob's descendants forever; his kingdom will never end." 34"How will this be," Mary asked the angel, "Since I am a virgin?" 35The angel answered, "The Holy Spirit will come on you, and the power of the Most High will overshadow you. So the holy one to be born will be called The Son of God. 36Even Elizabeth your relative is going to have a child in her old age, and she who was said to be unable to conceive is in her sixth month. 37For no word from God will ever fail." 38"I am the Lord's servant," Mary answered. "May your word to me be fulfilled?" Then the angel left her.

When people found out that Mary was pregnant, they did not believe that she became pregnant by the Holy Spirit. In any case, Joseph, did not believe her at first either, but God came to Him in a dream to let Him know that it was the will of God for her to be pregnant by the Holy Spirit. Meanwhile, Mary not only gave up her reputation but she gave up her name. She worshipped her God with reckless abandonment by abandoning her reputation and her will for the will of God.

In the meantime Mary thought about what the angel had said about her cousin, Elizabeth, being pregnant in her old age and Mary did not waste any time. She got up one morning and traveled to a town in Judah in the hill country, straight to Zachariah's house and greeted Elizabeth.

When Elizabeth heard Mary's greeting. The baby in the womb leaped.

She was filled with the Holy Spirit, and sang out with gladness. "Blessed are you among women, and blessed is the fruit of your womb." Elizabeth stated "why am I so favored, that the mother of the highest comes to me."

◄ TOUCH NOT MY ANOINTED

You see, Mary knew where to go where she would be celebrated, not just tolerated. Elizabeth understood what God had done in her and Mary's life. They both were pregnant with a purpose!

Mary went to the right person who would stimulate her and motivate her and who would help get her into alignment with her assignment. As you know, Mary's assignment was birthing the baby Jesus, the Son of the living God.

God set in motion the right person to encourage and edify and comfort her. Mary knew since Elizabeth was pregnant in her old age, they had something in common and then Mary felt relieved that the angel had told her the truth. In any event (3) three months later Elizabeth delivered a baby called John the Baptist who would later pave the way for the coming of Mary's child, Jesus, the Son of God. John the Baptist preached that all the people of Israel needed to repent from their sin and turn to God and be baptized. As John was finishing his ministry, he asked, "Do you think I am the Messiah? No, I am not! But He is coming soon and I'm not even worthy to be His slave and untie the sandals on His feet." Read the book of Luke to learn more about John, the Baptist.

Getting back to Mary. Eventually (after three months) she traveled back home and later delivered a beautiful baby boy named Jesus, the Son of God.

What a beautiful true story!! If you would like to read the whole story, it is also located in the Book of Luke 1:26-45

Consider this—Mary abandoned her life for the purpose of honoring God's request and she was not afraid. Why? Because I believe that she knew the will of God for this child was much greater than her fear of what people may think or do. She was not a people pleaser but a God pleaser. Listen to me, my beloved, in spite of the critic's tongue, whenever God tells you to do something, do not esteem lightly what he says. If you do, you will regret it and you will pay for it. However, he is a God who forgives and forgets. If you repent and ask Him to give you another opportunity to carry out that same assignment, He will honor your request. I hope as you read my book, you will have a glimpse of what my Father means to me.

When you have a revelation of your "Father's love," you can endure anything. You can abandon your desires for the desires of the King.

Every time I read about Mary, I am so amazed at how much she honored, loved, reverenced and obeyed her God with reckless abandonment. I believe the reason she was able to do this for God was because she had a revelation of her Father's love. She knew how much He loved her.

If you have the right picture of Jesus, it will drive your expectation of who He is and what He can do in your life.

◄ TOUCH NOT MY ANOINTED

What a powerful statement (I think I heard that statement from Graham Cooke).

My mind cannot compute what this young girl did and what she went through at such a young age. When God gives you an assignment, He does not just leave you hanging. He empowers you, equips you, anoints you and appoints you for the task; and He will set in motion the right people to help you carry it out like he did with Mary and Elizabeth and me.

Let's look at one more story in the Bible concerning worshiping God with reckless abandonment.

In 2 Samuel 6:12-14 (NIV) it says, "And the Ark of the Lord was brought up from the house of Obed-edom to the city of David with gladness. And David danced before the Lord with all his might." I pray that same worship will come upon you as you continue to read my book, as you worship and praise the Lord this very day with all of your heart. In Jesus' name, Amen.

Speaking of KING DAVID, I WOULD LIKE TO SPEAK ABOUT HIS LIFE AND HOW HE PROTECTED HIS "ANOINTING."

In 1 Samuel and 2 Samuel and Psalms, we read about David. Before I mention David, I guess I should tell you about Saul, whose reign preceded King David's. Paraphrasing, Saul was appointed the first king of Israel. Samuel was raised up to be a prophet. God and Samuel did not think that there should be a king over Israel because God (Himself) was king over Israel. However Israel begged for a king so God gave them what they desired. They wanted to be like all other nations. But God wanted them to be different. Yet God gave in to Israel's request on the condition that Israel would make God their ultimate ruler. God not only allowed Israel to have a king; but He (Himself) chose the man for the job. God asked Samuel (His prophet) to go and anoint Saul (the son of Kish) a man of the tribe of Benjamin, to be king and Saul reluctantly accepted the challenge. He reigned for forty years.

To make a long story short, Saul disobeyed God and he was rejected as king. In the meantime, God spoke to Samuel and asked him to stop crying over spilled milk and get up and anoint another king for Israel. God then asked Samuel to go and anoint one of Jesse's sons and Samuel did as the Lord requested. However, Samuel looked over seven of Jesse's sons and they were not God's choice. Samuel proceeded to ask Jesse if he had any more sons and he said, "Yes, my youngest. He takes care of the sheep." Samuel asked Jesse to go and get him and bring him to Him and they brought him in and the Lord told Samuel to anoint David as king, a man about whom God said, "I have found David, son of Jesse, a man after my own heart. He will do everything I want him to do."

Immediately afterward, Samuel filled the horn and anointed David as king and the Spirit of the Lord came upon David from that day forward. In the meantime, the Spirit of the Lord departed from Saul and an evil spirit troubled him. To make a long story short, Saul tried to kill David, even though Saul was still in the palace as king. For years, Saul was out to kill David because he knew that David would be the next king. In any event, while Saul and his men were looking to find and kill David, Saul decided to take a rest. He had pitched his tent in the hill of Hachilah. As Saul lay asleep in this place, David arose and came to the place where Saul and his guards were sleeping and Saul was not protected. Meanwhile, Abishai, who was with David, wanted to kill Saul. However David said, "Destroy him not, for who can stretch forth his hand against the Lord's anointed and be guiltless?" David also said that "the Lord forbid that I should stretch forth mine hand against the Lord's anointed." David honored the position that Saul held even though God rejected him as king. Consider this, David did not touch Saul because David wanted to protect his anointing by not committing sin against God's chosen vessel. However, time after time, David would pray a prayer asking God to deliver him from this pain, difficulty and hardship. One prayer he prayed was as follows: Psalm 86:1-5-(KJV):

"Bow down thou your ear, O Lord, hear my cry, for I am poor and needy. Preserve my soul; for I am holy. God, save me, save your servant that trusts in you. Be merciful unto me, O Lord, for I cry unto you daily. Rejoice the soul of your servant; for unto you, O Lord, do I lift up my soul. For you, Lord are good and ready to forgive and abundant in mercy unto all them that call upon you."

RECKLESS ABANDONEMENT

This was just one of the prayers that David prayed to God to rescue him from the hands of Saul. David was relentless in prayer to God to deliver him from the hands of Saul and from all of his enemies. However, God did not deliver him right away, for God was developing David's character and strengthening his faith. Although David went through difficulty, hardship and pain, he maintained a passionate love for God!! In his love for God, he held nothing back. David continued to worship God with reckless abandonment.

Sometimes I believe God allows you to go through things to purify your outcome, to make you more like His Son, Jesus.

Eventually, the Philistines fought against Israel (Saul's sons and his army) and the men of Israel fled from before the Philistines, and fell down slain in Mount Gilboa. The Philistines followed hard after Saul and his sons; and the Philistines slew Jonathan and all of Saul's sons. The battle went sore against Saul and the archers hit him and Saul was wounded. Therefore, Saul took a sword and fell upon it and died. So Saul died and his three sons and his armor bearer and all his men, that same day together. Saul died because he was unfaithful to the Lord. He failed to obey the Lord's command, and he even consulted a medium instead of asking the Lord for guidance. So Saul was killed and his kingdom was turned over to David, son of Jesse.

There is a lesson to be learned and it is, you do not go through things because of your past, but you go through

TOUCH NOT MY ANOINTED

things because of your future. David went through so much pain, difficulty and hardship to prepare him for being king. David survived the crises of many lives. Somehow he always bounced back and he always maintained a truly passionate love and devotion and trust in God. First and second Samuel does not give him a flawless character nor does it portray a perfect model for strength and courage. Like all of us, David had many weaknesses, and one of his weaknesses was Bathsheba, the wife of Uriah the Hittite. At the time that kings go to battle, King David stayed at home and as he rose from his bed and walked on his roof, he saw a woman washing herself and the woman was very beautiful. David sent for her and he lay with her and she became pregnant. To summarize, David had her husband (Uriah) killed in battle and later married Bathsheba. In any event, David finally acknowledged what he done, He asked God to forgive him and he poured his heart out to God and God forgave him. However, the baby Bathsheba was carrying by David, died as a direct result of His sin of having an affair with her and having her husband killed. Read the whole story about David and his kingdom and you will be amazed as well as intrigued and sometimes even appalled with the life of King David. He went from herding sheep to ruling a nation.

He appeals to his reader as he did to the Israelites. It seemed to me whatever he did, right or wrong, he did it with his whole heart. In his love for God, he always held nothing back. He was definitely a man after God's heart, passionately alive. In reading 1 Samuel, this book tells of David's youth and his long exile. 2 Samuel tells of David as a king, leading, inspiring and encouraging and uniting his people. Although he went through difficulty, hardship and pain, he allowed God to use him as a potter uses clay and David's character was developed and his faith was strengthened, preparing him to be king. At one point in his life, I believe that he realized that it was all about God and not about him. He was definitely not perfect, but he had a perfect heart toward God.

The Book of Psalms contains songs of joy and sadness. While these poems were written by a number of writers and poets, over half of these were credited to David, and I believe about one third of these Psalms are completely anonymous. Read the Book of Psalms and in almost every Psalm, you will experience the presence of God. You will see how much a difference He makes in our lives. You also will see the love that David had for His God.

Again, I believe because David had a revelation of his Father's love and he also had a true picture of God's image of Him. David realized that God was faithful to him when he was not faithful to God. In other words, because of this picture of the revelation of who God was, David could endure anything and David did!!

He always knew that God was actively involved in his situation and the kindness of God always sustained Him.

As I take this journey of life, I realize just how much my

◄ TOUCH NOT MY ANOINTED

Father loves me and it does not matter if anyone else loves me, I know that I have a revelation of my Father's love. This revelation of His love makes me immovable. My confidence in God can never be shaken and it governs my whole way of thinking!!! As time goes on, I have realized that the right picture and the right image and the right vision of who God is to me have driven my expectation of what He can do in my life (this bears repeating).

When you have a revelation of your Father's love, you can endure anything. I can think of the sparrows. They are cheap but not forgotten. (Matthew 10:29) When one sparrow falls to the ground, our Lord takes note of it. If God cares for the sparrow regardless of their value, how much more does He care for you?

Matthew 10:29—(NLT)
what is the price of two sparrows—one copper coin? But not a single sparrow can fall to the ground without your Father knowing it.

Beloved, If you do not know anything else, please know this= that God loves you; and beloved, rest in His love!!! Worship Him with reckless abandonment; abandon your desires for the desires of your king (Jesus).

Let me take this time to pray for you, beloved.

Father, I pray that you will give your people a revelation of who you are to them. Father, overwhelm them with your presence and take them into a deeper intimacy with you. Father, I pray that the cry of your people's heart is to know you in a deeper, more intimate way than they ever have before. Thank you, Father, that you will give them a divine acceleration of the longings in their heart for you at this very moment. Give them a vision of how much you truly love them and cause them to grasp just how much they need you, in Jesus' name I pray, Amen.

Let's take another look at the birds. Although God loves them dearly, does He deposit gifts and talents and potential and skills inside of them, anointing them to do what He called them to do? Of course not However, he has anointed us for a specific purpose giving up our desires for His. God desires so much for us to be like His Son, Jesus. He loves us that much!!

When you ask Jesus to come into your life, you have a new born-again Spirit and you die to yourself daily and you begin to renew your mind to line up with God's Word. As you renew your mind, God will stir up those gifts inside you and bring them to the surface. You will need to nurture them and develop them and cultivate them and mold them for your ministry. As you seek the Lord every day and develop an intimate relationship with God, He will anoint you to achieve more than what you can achieve alone and He will anoint you to do more than what you can do alone. In Jeremiah 29:11-NKJV it says, "These are the thoughts I think toward you, thoughts of peace and not evil, to give you a future and a hope." God will anoint you and appoint

◄ TOUCH NOT MY ANOINTED

you to carry out His will; and He promises you in Isaiah 41:10-11-(AMP) that He will be with you to help you and strengthen you and uphold you with His righteous right hand. "Fear not (there is nothing to fear) for I am with you: do not look around in terror and be dismayed, for I am your God. I will strengthen and harden you to difficulties. Yes, I will help you; yes, I will hold you up and retain you with my (victorious) right hand of rightness and justice. Behold, all they who are enraged and inflamed against you shall be put to shame and confounded; they who strive against you shall be as nothing and shall perish."

You see, this is what God does for His "anointed" (Touch Not My Anointed). And once you realize what He means to you, what you do for Him pales compared to what He does for you.

I have a question for you. Can there be any greater blessing than you abandoning your will to the will of God?

TOUCH NOT MY ANOINTED

I would like to share with you a true story concerning a person who touched God's anointed. I am at a point in my life that when someone mistreats me, I pray that God will have mercy and grace on them because I know that God takes note of everything that happens to me and to you, beloved. If you have asked Him into your life and your heart is surrendered to Him (if anyone bothers you) God will not let them get away with it. He is the God of Justice and He loves you and me with an eternal and an everlasting love. Because of His love for me and for His children, He will avenge our avengers and He always does!! In Psalm 145:20-(NKJV) it says the Lord protects (Preserves) those who love Him, and God knows that I really do love Him with all of my heart and He always (preserves) protects me.

I would like to give you an example of God fighting my battles.

I used to go to this store in Lansing, Michigan about three years ago, and the manager of this store did not seem to like me. Every time I walked into this store, she would intentionally look the other way, and when I asked her if she could let me into the dressing room, she would always ask the other lady to help me, even though she was not busy. This was not an isolated incident. This happened every single time I was in this store. I could not understand

TOUCH NOT MY ANOINTED

what I had done to her and I wanted to ask her, but I did not. However, I eventually decided not to go in that store anymore and I prayed to God that she would not treat any other person like she had treated me. I also prayed that God would extend to her not what she deserved (justice) but I asked that He extend to her mercy and grace. After I stopped going to this store, months later, I happened to be walking by the store one day and I noticed a sign on the door that said "going out of business sale." Suddenly, it hit me like a tidal wave that this store that I once loved so much was now going out of business. I walked into the store and there she was. The same lady who ignored me before, rushed over and asked me if she could help me find something. I immediately asked her why the store was going out of business. She looked at me, almost a stare, and said that they hardly ever had any business any more. She said people just stopped coming in, so therefore, they were not making any profits. She asked me to let her know if I wanted to try on anything and she would be more than happy to help me. First of all, I was so surprised that they did not have much business, because before I stopped going there, the store was always full of people. Everybody went to that store because the prices were so reasonable. Everybody that I knew shopped in that store and they loved it. Although I had not been in that store for several months, it was one of my favorite stores to shop in. I asked her if she would be transferred to another location and she said they could not find a place to put her. She also mentioned that they did not give her much notice. I could not believe this same lady who seemed not to like me before now seemed drawn to me. I could not look around the store to shop because she needed someone to listen to her and I guess I was it. She was devastated about being let go on such short notice. I felt so sorry for her but I was not sure why she felt the need to tell me every detail of what happened. However, I stood there and listened and I gave her some encouraging words to comfort her. Eventually, I had a chance to look around in the store and she once again came over to me and stated that she would give me two for the price of one. I was looking at a beautiful top and I asked her the price and she stated that whatever I had, she would take it and give me two for the price of one. I gave her five dollars for two beautiful tops. I am reminded of God's Word. He said that He will give you double for your trouble and that was what God did. I received two tops for the sale price of one. (Actually the sale price for the one top was eight dollars and forty nine cents but she gave it to me for two for five dollars!! What a blessing from God. God repaid me two blessings for my trouble!!

"...TODAY I DECLARE THAT I WILL RESTORE TO YOU DOUBLE.

—ZECH. 9:12 RSV

It was almost like she was apologizing to me for the way she had treated me in the past. You see, I believe that God had somehow changed her heart toward me because He takes it personally when our feelings get hurt for no reason at all. I believe that God had given her a dream and I was in it. I believe that in this dream, He let her know that she treated me very badly for no reason.

I also believe that she was reaping the fruit of her own ways and got caught in the trap of her own schemes. It does not pay to be unkind to anyone because you reap what you sow. She sowed bad seed so she reaped a bad harvest of losing her job. However, I prayed that she would get another job and this job would be even better than the one she had lost. I told her that God would repay her double for her trouble. I could be wrong, but I believe that this sales lady repented and I also believe that she was sorry for the way she treated me in the past. I believe that she had true repentance.

You have to understand that God sees everything, everything is naked and exposed in His sight, and God hates injustice. When God sees that someone is mistreating you, His anointed, He does not take it lightly. In Geneses 12:3—(NKJV) God says this about the Israelites: He said that He will bless those who bless them, and He will curse those who curse them. When I read this verse, I put my name in this verse also. Although I am not Jewish, I have asked Jesus into my life and I became grafted into His Jewish family. So whatever God says about the Jewish people, I claim that for me!!! You see, no one can curse me and get away with it, absolutely no one!!! I am not proud, but I am very confident of how much my God loves me and I have faith in His promises. Whatever He says, I believe it because God does not lie and He watches over His word to perform it. I trust God! **Again, I say, I trust God.**

If I may, I would like to share another testimony with you. This testimony is concerning a family member who has a son who literally hated me. I always believed that he was emotionally and mentally challenged and in need of major therapy. He was indeed an angry little boy and still is, I believe, an angry young man.

However, every time I went to visit her, her son would put forth an effort to let me know how much he hated me. The only reason I could come up with is that he was jealous of my relationship with her. I think I can understand a little bit of how he felt, for he had no one else but his mom and when he was small, he was sexually abused, and on top of that his father was an absentee dad. He never really had a father figure or any man with character around to teach him how to become a man. I believe if his father had come around and helped him, he would not have turned into this angry young man. Although I tried so hard to build a relationship with him myself when he was just a little boy, he did not accept it. It seemed the more I tried to make a connection, to be his aunt or even his friend, the more he hated me. I remember when he was a little boy, I would buy him almost anything that he wanted. I wanted to give him special attention because he never really knew his dad. He was always so hard on his toys and when I bought him things, he would break them the same day. Eventually, I had a talk with him and I told him if he continued to be abusive to the toys that I bought him, I would no longer buy him any more toys. As I look back, I believe because his dad was not around, he took his anger out on all his toys. Every toy that he had, he would break them and he seemed to get enjoyment out of doing it. Apparently, he was carrying around hidden hurts such as bitterness, unforgiveness, anger and rejection. Incidentally, my sister and I took him for therapy quite often and it did not seem to help. He had years of therapy, but to no avail.

However, as he became older, I did at one point have the privilege of leading him to the Lord more than once, but I am not sure if his heart was yielded for I never saw any fruit. In any event, every time I would go to visit my sister, he (who was about 18 years old or older) would threaten me by motioning to slit my throat. He would do this almost every time I visited her. In any event, one day I was over at her house and he looked at me and once again motioned that he was going to slit my throat with his hand. However this time, I told him that if he continued to threaten me, I would call the police on him (although I would not have done that). Nevertheless, he laughed in my face and stated that he would call the police himself and have me talk to them. He then proceeded to do just that. He called the police and gave the phone to me and I did not accept it. However, immediately, the police arrived at my sister's house and her son answered the door and proceeded to let the police officers in. The police asked who made the call and this young man admitted that it was he who made the call. As time went on, the police continued to ask him ques-

TOUCH NOT MY ANOINTED

tions and right away, the police looked at me and asked me if I wanted to file charges against this young man and I said no. In any event, I believe that they came to the conclusion after questioning him that he was mentally unstable and he could possibly hurt someone or even hurt himself. So therefore, they felt like they had enough evidence by talking to him, to take him downtown and arrest him.

You see, in the Bible it says a fool's mouth is his destruction and his lips are a snare of his soul. In Proverbs 18: 7-(KJV) It also says that the mouth of fools are their ruin.

As you see, it was this young man who called the police and the police ended up taking him downtown and arresting him. This was only the beginning of a lifelong battle. Since this time, he's been on medication and was diagnosed with a mental illness. That one call forever marked his entire life. Once again, I believe that God came to my rescue and protected me from evil. Even today, the medication that this young man is on does not deter him from still hating me with a passion. Not only does he hate me, but he also believes that I am responsible for him being on medication. He has always and still is operating on false data.

From what I understand, he will be on this medication for the rest of his life. However, I believe if he rededicated his life to the Lord and renewed his mind and had an intimate relationship with the Lord, I truly believe that he would be healed and delivered and set free from this sickness and disease. Why? Because that is God's promise. In Jeremiah 30:17-(NKJV) it says, "I will restore health unto you and I will heal you of your wounds." Also Matt. 10: 8-(NKJV) says, "God told the disciples to go and heal the sick, cleanse the lepers, raise the dead and cast out demons." Jesus came so that we can have abundant life and Jesus wants this young man to be free, and so do I. Read John 10: 10-(NKJV).

I continue to pray for this young man and I believe that God is going to move in his life powerfully. I have not kept in touch with him or his mom, but other family members keep me up-to-date on the status of his location and his whereabouts.

I would like to say to him that I still love you and I always will. You will always be a prince to me. I would like to pray for him. I speak this prophetic word over his life.

For now, I will just call him Ken (not his real name). I pray he will be a tree planted by the rivers of waters and in due season, he will bear fruit and his leaves will not wither and everything he touches will prosper. Father, I pray that you will give him a dream, let this dream be so vivid, so clear, so powerful and so inescapable that it will be impossible for him to miss what you are saying to him. Father, overwhelm his heart with your presence so that everything he thinks and does will be governed by you. Father, cause those hidden hurts such as bitterness, unforgiveness, anger and rejection be released and replace them with your love, patience, kindness, gentleness and self—control; and Father, put in place your purpose and your plans in his life.

I ask, Father, for a divine acceleration to speed up this process.

Father, you said that you hold the heart of a king in your hand and you can turn it any way you will. Father, turn Ken's heart, cause him to make decisions according to your will and not according to his. In Jesus' Name, Amen.

Beloved, I know that I've spent a lot of time praying for Ken but I believe God orchestrated every word of it.

ANN'S HISTORY

A Flood of Memories

For now, I would like to turn back the hands of time and tell you more about my life before I was saved. This is my history, not my testimony.

When I lived in Tennessee, I was sheltered not only as a child, but as a teenager and a young adult. I did not care. I did not know what it was like to go out with a guy, but then I came to Michigan and I married the first guy I dated. His name was George. I did not even love him for I did not know what love was. However, this marriage did not last very long. The first week we were married, he was seeing other women and when I approached him with this unfaithfulness, he said if I did not like it, there is the door. So after being married to him for three months, I left and I moved back down south to Tennessee with Mom and Dad. Weeks later, he drove down south to come and get me, but I begged Dad not to let him in and Dad obeyed my wishes. I was so frightened if Dad let him in, I was so fearful that my parents would have made me agree to go back to Michigan with Him. He was very charming and very believable when he spoke. He had a way with words.

He was almost thirty and I had just finished high school. I was young and naive.

In any event, my mom thought that I should at least talk to him since he drove all those miles to come and get me. However, that did not happen, thanks to my dad. Eventually he drove back to Michigan without even seeing me. He was not a kind man. I really do not know why he married me for he did not love me nor I him.

He loved women, not just one but many.

I stayed in Tennessee for about one year and I eventually moved back to Michigan and we were later divorced. Let me reiterate. George loved women, not just one but many. From what I understand, based on reliable sources, he was married at least five more times after we were divorced. However, years later, he eventually passed away suddenly. When I found out that he had died, I do not even think that I mourned his death and I did not go to the funeral. After all, I hardly knew him, although he was once my husband. However, as I think back, I wish I would have at least gone to the funeral.

In any event, I do not know what happened to me immediately after our divorce. I became a wild animal stalking its prey. I was somebody totally different. At this time I was in my twenties and I began to have a fast-paced life, as you will read later. I really changed drastically. I dated not only one man but sometimes two at a time. I would date brothers and even best friends. I felt happy when I saw them fighting over me. It made me feel important. My mom would have been shocked, to say the least, if she had seen me acting that way. I became someone that I did not know. In 1973, when I was about twenty-four, my mom passed to heaven. She was about 52 or 53 years old. I was beyond devastated! Her death hit me like a tidal wave all at once and it was almost too much for me to bear. I never felt this kind of pain before and I haven't since! It was beyond me what I needed to do, so I just suffered in silence.

It took me forever to get over it. I cried for days and I could not hold back my tears (even now I still hurt when I think of her). I was so hurt and I did not know how to handle this pain since I did not know God, so I basically just continued in my sin. Instead of mourning my mom's death, I began dating even more. I wanted to forget this pain so I would go out with three or four men in one week. I was hurting but no one knew it but me and God, and late at night, I would cry myself to sleep.

Eventually, I believe that God began to talk to me in His Word as I was led to pick up the Bible and I was covered in shame. I knew I was doing wrong and I was being convicted big time. As you read on, I will give you details of what happened.

"BUT IN MY SIN, GOD STILL LOVED ME."

One day as I was in my one-bedroom apartment in Michigan, I was thinking about my life and how it had been so meaningless. I thought about how I was living by my flesh and doing what my feelings governed me to do and yet I was unhappy. I was so lonely and so restless and I had no peace. My heart seemed to long for something, but I was not sure what it was. Whatever I was longing for was painful and I cried longing for it. So I said in my heart, 'as it happens to fools, it also happens to me.' Eventually, I looked in the corner of my room and I saw a Bible and I do not even know where it came from. I picked it up, which was very unusual for me at this time. I did not even remember having a Bible. I turned the pages and I came upon Jeremiah 2:21, 23b, 24a-(NLT) and He began to speak to me in His Word as if He was recalling a distant memory.

"BUT I WAS THE ONE WHO PLANTED YOU, CHOOSING A VINE OF PUREST STOCK—THE VERY BEST. HOW DID YOU GROW INTO THIS CORRUPT WILD VINE? FACE THE AWFUL SINS YOU HAVE DONE. YOU ARE LIKE A RESTLESS FEMALE CAMEL SEARCHING FOR A MATE. YOU ARE LIKE A WILD DONKEY SNIFFING THE WIND AT MATING TIME. WHO CAN RESTRAIN YOUR LUST?"

TOUCH NOT MY ANOINTED

As I read and continued to read, the tears flowed down my face and I began to cry out loud for it was as if He was speaking directly to me (Jeremiah 3:19-NLT).

"I THOUGHT TO MYSELF, I WOULD LOVE TO TREAT YOU AS MY OWN CHILDREN!" I WANTED NOTHING MORE THAN TO GIVE YOU THIS BEAUTIFUL LAND-THE FINEST POSSESSION IN THE WORLD. I LOOK FORWARD TO YOU CALLING ME "FATHER" AND I WANTED YOU NEVER TO TURN FROM ME."

Philippians 4:8-(NIV)

"FINALLY MY BROTHERS AND SISTERS, FIX YOUR THOUGHTS ON WHAT IS TRUE, AND HONORABLE, AND RIGHT, AND PURE, AND LOVELY AND ADMIRABLE. THINK ABOUT THINGS THAT ARE EXCELLENT AND WORTHY OF PRAISE. KEEP PUTTING INTO PRACTICE ALL YOU HAVE LEARNED AND RECEIVED FROM ME—EVERYTHING YOU HEARD FROM ME AND SAW ME DOING. THEN THE GOD OF PEACE WILL BE WITH YOU."

As I began to hold back my tears, I realized that the God of this universe was speaking to me in His word and going out of His way to get my attention. All of a sudden, I could not think straight. My heart was pounding and I could not process what I just read. I walked to my balcony and sat there with my mouth open and I could not ascertain what I just read. I sat for a while and I went back into my apartment. When I went to my room, I felt a beautiful presence and I thought back on all the words that I believe God had spoken to me as I was reading His word. My heart was pounding and I could not think straight and I could not understand or process what God was saying to me in His word. For hours, I slowly, cautiously and carefully meditated on every word. I was numb and I could not believe what I thought I was hearing. I was torn between two impulses—the urge to run and forget what I believed God was saying to me or to continue to read and hear what He had to say. I was frozen and I did not know what to do. I knew deep within me that His word was not only a message but it was a warning and yet I wanted to run from the truth.

Again, His truth was flooding my heart with light and all I could do was cry but even then the tears seemed to mean nothing to me because it did not stop me from doing what Satan was leading me to do. As I look back now, I was so blind and yet I could see, and so deaf yet could hear. But I could only see and hear what the world wanted me to see. God's words alone were truth but I was not only unwilling, I was unable to let His words discipline me. It was as if I understood them but I would not take heed to what He was saying to me. It was as if I was trapped in a prison with locks on the door and I could not escape. No matter how much of the truth that I heard, my mind seemed unmovable, rigid and inflexible to the Word of God.

I realize now the reason why I was so bound up in this

TOUCH NOT MY ANOINTED

world was because in God's word (which I learned later) said "You are of your father the devil, and the desires of your father you want to do" John 8:44-(NKJV). That is the reason why we need to be born again (asking Jesus in our heart) so Jesus can be our father, not Satan and we can hear God speaking to us and we can obey.

Seeing how I was not saved at that time, I was listening to Satan, not God. What a tragedy!!!

It was as if I wanted to obey God's Word but I could not. It was as if the hold on me was so strong, I could not shake it. Why? Because I was God's creation but I was not His child. You see, when Adam and Eve committed the sin of listening to the serpent in the garden and obeying him instead of obeying God, we were all born in sin, which separates us from God and aligns us with Satan as God's enemy. Because of the fall of Adam and Eve in the garden, we have to ask Jesus into our lives in order to be His child. Read Genesis 3, Ephesians 2:3-10 and Romans 9:8.

As I was reading God's Word in my room, it was as if God Himself had entered into my room and was speaking directly to me. I was now sitting in the dark since the day had turned to night. I did not know why He felt that it was so important for me to know what He had to say. I began to cry again and I could not make myself stop. It was as if I was no longer in charge of my tears. I remember it was late at night and all I could think about was His words. His words were almost inescapable.

"BUT IN MY SIN, GOD STILL LOVED ME."

It was beyond me how the God of this universe could love someone like me so deeply.

I realized more than before that I lived in a world that is ruled by Satan and not only ruled by Satan, but he is the god of this world. This is not to say that he rules the world completely; God is still sovereign. But I believe it does mean, in God's infinite wisdom, He has allowed Satan to operate in this world within boundaries that He has set before him.

I found out later that when the Bible says Satan has power over this world, we must remember that God has given him control over unbelievers only. Believers are no longer under the authority of Satan. At this time, I was not saved so Satan had tremendous power over me. The bottom line is the unsaved follow Satan's agenda and I was the unsaved.

No matter what God was saying to me, I was continuing to be loyal to Satan. I refused over and over again to listen to God's Word although his words were flooding my heart with truth and with light. My heart and my mind was continuing to be rebellious and I was continuing to live my life my way and not God's way. It was almost as if my heart had hardened. However, I believe that the god of this world has blinded the mind of unbelievers so they cannot see the light of the Gospel of the Glory of Christ. See 2 Corinthians 4:4.

Looking back, I can see now why I kept making wrong

choices. Why? Because I was following the wrong person, and going down the wrong path. I was deceived by the deceiver.

I continued to be so deep in my sin, dating and spending nights with men I did not even know and I did not even seem to care. It was as if I had spiritual amnesia. I would read His word and the next minute I would be in bed with a stranger. If you had looked up sin in the Bible, my picture would have been there in full bloom.

As I was getting ready for bed, my eyes kept looking at the Bible as if God Himself had summoned me to read it. Although it was late, I once again picked up the Bible and I held it in my hand. Although I held it in my hand, I was afraid to open it for fear of once again hearing the truth. I remember when I was a child, my mom would always say "you shall know the truth and the truth shall set you free." Consequently, I knew the truth but I was not ready nor willing to be set free. Although I was reading God's Word, at that time I was listening to the voice that spoke the loudest, the voice of my father, the devil! What a tragedy!!!

I WAS SOMEWHAT IN A DAZE AND I COULD NOT CONCENTRATE FOR I KNEW THAT I HAD AN EXPERIENCE WITH GOD. THE GOD OF ABRAHAM, ISAAC AND JACOB, THE GOD THAT MY MOM KNEW WHEN I WAS A CHILD.

I finally fell off to sleep and the next morning, when I woke

"BUT IN MY SIN, GOD STILL LOVED ME."

up, the Bible was still in my hand. Although this was an experience I will never forget, I was still not ready nor willing to come to him. Like the Israelites, I was proud and rebellious and stubborn and paid no attention to His words. I refused to obey Him. I was like a lamb being led to slaughter by an evil force and I did not seem to care!

I think of all the miracles and favor he bestowed upon me when I was younger and yet I still walked in my own way and not God's way. I got up from my bed and looked into the mirror and I felt a sense of shame. I thought to myself, "How can I continue in my evil against God after He has literally spoken to me in His word and literally come to me in visions and dreams to warn me of trouble ahead? But even now, I know from my experience with the Lord, that He is so forgiving and gracious and merciful, slow to anger and rich in unfailing love.

Although I had not obeyed Him, I know that He would not abandon me. What an amazing God!!!

I then asked myself, "What is it going to take for me to be fully persuaded that God is all I need?"

Nevertheless, I realized that at this time, Satan was my father and I was listening to his voice. I needed to be saved but I did not know it.

What was it going to take for me to turn and go His direction? Why was it so hard for me to do what I knew is right?

◄ TOUCH NOT MY ANOINTED

I had so many questions and yet I did not want to hear His answers.

At any rate, I did realize something and it was that God was not ever going to give up on me even if I had given up on myself. Once again I picked up the Bible and I believe that God prompted me to turn to Psalm 32:8-9-(NLT):

THE LORD SAYS, "I WILL GUIDE YOU ALONG THE BEST PATHWAY FOR YOUR LIFE. I WILL ADVISE YOU AND WATCH OVER YOU. DO NOT BE LIKE A SENSELESS HORSE OR MULE THAT NEEDS A BIT AND A BRIDLE TO KEEP IT UNDER CONTROL."

As I was reading this verse, I was so amazed how God is so real. Once again, I was speechless. There was not one word in the English language to even scratch the surface of what I was feeling. Nevertheless, I did realize one thing and it was that I was like that senseless horse that needed a bit and a bridle to keep me on track. In a sense I was more corrupt than the mule and the horse. I felt that even a bit and a bridle could not have tamed me. I was, in my own mind, not to be tamed.

In any event, I remember a couple of days later, I got the urge and was compelled to pick up the Bible again when I was at home in my room. I opened up the Bible and I believe that I was led back to Jeremiah 3:19-(NLT)

I WOULD LOVE TO TREAT YOU AS MY CHILDREN! I

"BUT IN MY SIN, GOD STILL LOVED ME."

WANTED NOTHING MORE TO GIVE YOU THIS BEAUTIFUL LAND-THE FINEST POSSESSION IN THE WORLD. I LOOKED FORWARD TO YOUR CALLING ME FATHER AND I WANTED YOU NEVER TO TURN FROM ME."

As I continued to read, I realized that He had given me this verse twice.

As I continued to read, I believe that I was led to these Scriptures below.

Jeremiah 6:16-(NLT)

"THIS IS WHAT THE LORD SAYS:

STOP AT THE CROSSROADS AND LOOK AROUND. ASK FOR THE GODLY WAYS AND ASK FOR THE ANCIENT PATH AND WALK IN IT. TRAVEL ITS PATH, AND YOU WILL FIND REST FOR YOUR SOULS.

The Lord continued to speak to me through His word in Jeremiah 33:3-(NKJV):

"CALL TO ME AND I WILL ANSWER YOU AND I WILL SHOW YOU GREAT AND MIGHTY THINGS, WHICH YOU DO NOT KNOW."

Jeremiah 29:11-13—(NKJV) "FOR I KNOW THE THOUGHTS THAT I THINK TOWARD YOU, SAYS THE LORD, THOUGHTS OF PEACE AND NOT OF EVIL, TO

◄ TOUCH NOT MY ANOINTED

GIVE YOU A FUTURE AND A HOPE. THEN YOU WILL CALL UPON ME AND GO PRAY TO ME, AND I WILL LISTEN TO YOU AND YOU WILL SEEK ME AND FIND ME WHEN YOU SEARCH FOR ME WITH ALL OF YOUR HEART. I WILL BE FOUND BY YOU, SAYS THE LORD, AND I WILL BRING YOU BACK FROM YOUR CAPTIVITY."

I felt God speaking directly to me again and leading me to those Scriptures. I picked up my purse and left my apartment and I went on a long walk trying to take in all that He had said to me. I guess I could not understand how it is that God is wanting me to want him so much. There was a bench where I was walking and I sat down for a moment and I looked at all the people that were walking by me and I wondered if God was trying to reach them also. Some man came and sat by me and he had a bottle in his hand (beer) and he looked at me as if to say, "Are you lonely too?" Yes, I was lonely and empty and I needed God in my life for I had no peace and no guidance. I was so desperate to have good friends, something I had never experienced. Actually I would have settled for just one friend, someone I could just talk to.

I sat for a while and I left and went back home. After having these experiences with God, I never really was the same. Although I did not stop having sex altogether, I would only date one man at a time, which was an improvement for me. I knew one thing and that was God loved me enough to pursue me; and this was the first time in my life that I felt an unconditional love from anyone. I knew that I was

"BUT IN MY SIN, GOD STILL LOVED ME."

His creation, but at this time, I was still not His child; and I knew beyond a shadow of a doubt that He loved me with all of His heart. However, even though I would still date, the relationship I had was shallow. Although I continued to have a sexual relationship with my boyfriend, I would never enjoy it because I would feel guilty. I knew after the experience I had with God, that God had something more for me and all I had to do was to make a choice, make a conscious decision and stick with it, but yet, I was still in defiance. As time went on, I dated less and less, but I still...

Craved attention from the wrong source and rejected attention from the right source.

I used to ask myself, how could I reject someone who only wanted nothing but the best for me?

God would give me life and life more abundantly. He would give me love and value and peace and contentment; He was the right source and yet I continued to reject Him. I was so unhappy with the world and yet continued to live the world's way. I continued to sleep around but only with the man that I was seeing at the time, unlike before, when I would date two men at once, sometimes even more. I would go out with one man one night and the next night, I would date a different one. After I did this, I always felt abused, abandoned and rejected. I felt as though I was a piece of trash trying to find my way home. I remember one night lying in bed wondering how I came to this place in my life, a place of deception and instability and self-hatred. I remember sometimes when

◄ TOUCH NOT MY ANOINTED

I used to go to my mom complaining about something, she would say, "This too will pass." It always gave me comfort when I remembered those words and it still does.

I continued to ask myself 'what is wrong with me?' It was as if I was preordained and destined for destruction. I was blind and could not see and deaf and could not hear. When God spoke through His word, I listened but did not understand nor did I comprehend it—and if I did understand it, I pretended not to. However later on, I realized that it was almost impossible for me to respond to God's Word because I did not have the Holy Spirit inside me to guide me in doing what was right.

I was ruled by my flesh. What a terrible tragedy. I was also listening to the voice of the enemy telling me that I was no good and I did not deserve anything good. I believe that the enemy knew that I had a huge call on my life and he did everything he knew to do to stop me, to block me, to hinder me and hold me back; and it continued to work because I continued to listen to him because I still was not saved.

As I think back, when God was speaking to me through His Word, I learned what God was really like. I sensed that He wanted me to really know Him. He wanted me to rest in Him and He wanted me to know who He is and how much He loved me.

I used to wonder why I did not have dreams or visions any-

"BUT IN MY SIN, GOD STILL LOVED ME."

more like I did when I was younger. At some point, they left.

If I did not get anything else from His word, I knew without a shadow of a doubt, just how much God loved me.

Through all of my sin, He let me know that He would never give up on me. I realized then, as I realize now, God was in this for the long haul. God is so faithful. He is so consistent and I knew that He would never ever give up on me. I believe that God wanted me to rest in Him and to love Him. He wanted me to see Him for who He is, and who He wanted me to be in His life. God is so good! God is so kind—like Graham Cooke said, "He is relentlessly kind to me, He is the kindest person I know and He is the kindest person I will ever know." I remember all the evil things that I was doing and yet He came after me with love, and kindness and compassion. He loved me that much! In His word, it said: To whom little is forgiven, this person loves little and the one who is forgiven much, loves much. Luke 7:36-50 NKJV—A Sinful Woman Forgiven—Then one ...

A Sinful Woman **Forgiven**—Then one of the Pharisees asked Him to eat with him. And He went ... [47] Therefore I say to you, her sins, which are many, are **forgiven**, for she **loved much.** But to **whom little is forgiven**, the same **loves little.**" [48]

My life today, I have been forgiven for so much and I love much and I have to learn to forgive much. God is so faithful and He is forever unchanging. I love Him, I truly love Him much! When he came to me when I was heavy in my sin, He did not judge me, but He loved me through it all!! In Hosea 2: 14—15a,b,-(NKJV) it reads:

"THEREFORE I WILL ALLURE HER, WILL BRING HER INTO THE WILDERNESS AND SPEAK COMFORT TO HER, I WILL GIVE HER VINEYARDS FROM THERE, AND THE VALLEY OF A'CHORA AS A DOOR OF HOPE, AND SHE SHALL SING THERE, AS IN THE DAYS OF HER YOUTH.

Also, I believe He led me to this verse in the Bible and I began to read it Jeremiah 5:14-(NLT):

"Because the people are talking like this, my message will flame out of your mouth and burn the people like kindling wood."

I could not begin to understand this verse at that time, so I just pondered it in my heart day after day.

You see what God did. I was sinning and He allured me in the wilderness and He spoke comfort to me and not only did he comfort me with His word, but I truly believe that He gave me a message about my future. I remember kneeling on the floor and praying to my mom's God as sometimes I did and I asked Him to help me to understand what I am supposed to do and how I am to do it. I then asked Him to forgive me for being so stupid. This is what I believe that He said to me once again:

"BUT IN MY SIN, GOD STILL LOVED ME."

"Ann, I love you as I love my first born Israel. You are my hidden treasure and I take great delight in you and I will quiet you with my love and I will always rejoice over you with my singing."

This is the same verse that He gave me once before and I treasured it.

I believe that I also heard Him say to my heart, Hebrews 10:30a, 31:

"I will take revenge, I will pay them back, I will deal with them. I will judge my own people. "

I was kind of puzzled at that time, for I knew not what this meant. Then it hit me like a ton of bricks. I realized it was almost like He was speaking into my future. It was as if He was declaring and decreeing life over me and my future.

I cried, for I knew I was still not ready to obey, although I wanted to. I cried for almost the whole day and His love flooded me with His presence and I was overwhelmed with His peace.

I could not understand the revelation of God's love for me, for it was almost more than I could handle.

I asked myself, what was it going to take for me to change?

It was the enemy speaking in my ear telling me not to listen

to God, but to listen to him. However, I not only was listening to the enemy, I was listening to me. I was also responsible for making these wrong decisions.

I realized back then as well as now, that it was me making these wrong choices.

Satan is deceptive, crafty, subtle, and cunning and he is the father of lies. When you do not know God, you do not have His Spirit to guide you and that is what happened with me. I made a choice to continue in my sin, but I was gradually changing. I did not despise small beginnings. I was trying to be better; but I needed to ask God into my life but I didn't know how. If I knew how, He would send the Holy Spirit to come alongside of me to help me. The Holy Spirit would lead me to all truth. I knew that I could not change on my own because I needed God to help me. At this time in my life, I did not know what I needed to do.

A MOMENT OF CLARITY

As time passed, I met a man with whom I fell in love. We lived together for years although we did not get married. I dated him and him only. His name was Harvey. Unfortunately, I became pregnant more than once and he and I went to the abortion clinic to talk to someone and they convinced me on several occasions that although I was pregnant, the embryos were not alive yet and I believed them. Yes, I had a few abortions and I am not proud of it. Even now when I think of it, tears come! I realize now that I was deceived! After I had an abortion, I used to mourn and I did not understand why, seeing how there was no life in my womb, why would I mourn? Now I know that there was life in my womb and I was totally deceived and my babies' lives were taken needlessly. Talking about this is still a little hard for me but I know they are in good hands.

Since I have asked God into my life, my God has forgiven me! My babies are in heaven with the Lord! I am forgiven! Once I asked God into my life, God and I talked for weeks about my babies and I know now that I made a huge mistake but I have to believe that God understands and He does forgive me so I have forgiven myself.

Let me get back to Harvey, the love of my life. One of the biggest issues that we had was that he could not keep a job. He would work for a second and then he would quit.

◄ TOUCH NOT MY ANOINTED

I knew that I had to leave him in order to keep my sanity. Our relationship was comfortable and familiar and sometimes fun. But it was also sick, dysfunctional, and diseased. He smoked on a regular basis and saw nothing wrong with smoking pot. His addiction to this drug marijuana eventually drew me in. I felt trapped and I knew that our relationship was not going anywhere. Although we had many good times and we loved one another, I knew that I wanted more for my life. I knew that I had to leave and I wanted to do it quickly before I changed my mind.

I moved away from him without him knowing where I was going. I knew that in order to have a productive life, I needed to leave. I moved from Lansing to Okemos. I felt a sense of accomplishment. I did not feel like I wanted to move, but I believe that I was compelled to move by a higher source. It was as if I was doing this without my full consent. I cannot really explain it. I was not sure how I did it, but I did it. It was one of the hardest things that I knew I had to do. At some point, I was glad that I moved away, but I still missed him. I was torn between two responses. Every day, he was always on my mind and I wanted so desperately to see him. However, I wanted desperately to forget him and move on with my life. As time went on, I felt that was actually beginning to happen. Months later, one morning I heard a knock on my door. I looked through the peephole and saw that it was Harvey. I was immediately torn between two impulses—I was surprised and happy to see him, but at the same time I wanted to run and hide and not let him in the door. I was still very much in love with him and yet, I knew that opening the door would not be the right thing to do. However, I opened the door. I didn't ask him how he found me. I was just so happy to see him again. After I opened the door we hugged each other and I began to cry. I explained to him why I felt that I had to leave him. I was so glad to see him but I could tell that he was holding on to unforgiveness toward me for leaving him. He could not understand how I could have moved away from him after being with him for so many years. I tried to explain to him why I had to leave but no matter what I said, it would not satisfy him. In the meantime he took my face in his hand and he said that he had something very important to ask me. He looked at me without blinking his eye and he had a serious expression on his face and he kissed me on my forehead. At that point, I did not know what to say or what to do because I recognized that look. It used to always frighten me. I was reluctant to know what that expression meant; nevertheless, I was very curious as to what he had to say. Immediately, without a beat, he said that he wanted me to do something with him that would be a beautiful high beyond my belief. He also stated that if we did it together, we would be together forever and no one would be able to separate us from one another. At this point, I did not like the sound of it and I was not sure if I wanted to hear the rest of it. However, he continued. He began to speak slowly, cautiously, and carefully deliberating very word. He said that he wanted me to promise him that I would do it before he told me what it was. His tone was tense and slightly sarcastic. The more he talked, the more I wanted to run from him. I was becoming very uncomfortable. Eventually, he seemed to sense that I

◄ TOUCH NOT MY ANOINTED

was not very excited nor was I looking forward to what he had to say. He pulled me onto his lap and he promised me that he would never, ever ask me to do anything that would hurt me or jeopardize our relationship. As he continued to talk, I was beginning to be more scared than ever before. He asked me to put my trust in him and him alone. Tears were beginning to flow out of my eyes and I could not stop crying. He looked at me and told me how much he missed me and he wanted us to always be together. Finally, I asked him with tears running down my eyes, what did he want me to do with him? Without hesitation, he said that he had some crack cocaine and he wanted to snort it with me. He pleaded with me over and over again. He said that would make him happy. I realized at that very moment that Harvey had really changed and it was not a good change. I did not know who this person was. Although I still loved him, I could not do what he asked me to do. He continued to plead with me and all of a sudden, I cried so loud that he finally stopped asking me. In the back of my mind, I realized that he was hooked on cocaine and he could not stop and he wanted me to be hooked also.

He was addicted to drugs and I did not know how to help him. It was almost like he wanted us to do this drug and we would die together. I heard years ago that if you obey Satan, he will then try to kill you and I believe this was the case. Satan wanted me dead but God had better plans and God's plans always succeed.

Finally, Harvey gave up trying to persuade me to do the

drugs and I pleaded with him over and over again not to do it, but it was too late. He was already hooked. After he finished using the drugs, I tried to talk to him, but he fell asleep. I went upstairs and got a blanket and laid it over him. I lay right beside him and I cried all night. I could not stop myself from crying. I realized that the love of my life was hooked on crack and I did not know what to do. I was not sure why it was so critical for me to snort the drugs with him, but it seemed as if it was life or death to him. When Harvey woke up the next morning, I was still lying on the couch beside him and he looked at me as if to say, "Ann, help me." I took his face in my hand and I promised him that I would help him get help. Again, my heart was pounding and I could not process what was happening. I told him that I would do what I had to do to help him to get delivered from this drug. I told him that I would look in the yellow pages and do what I had to do to get him the help that he needed. I also told him that I was going to find him immediate help. He did not respond. I believe deep down he knew he needed help but he did not want it because he was addictive. He looked at me and said that he was not an addict and he did not need help. The more I tried to help him, the more he pushed me away. It was like beating a dead horse. He would not listen. He did not want my help. I realized that I could not help him because he did not want it. In order for you to get help, you have to accept the fact that you need help and he would not acknowledge it.

What do you do when everything you try has absolutely

TOUCH NOT MY ANOINTED

no influence on the person you love, which reminded me of God trying to help me.

Everything I tried, no matter what I said or did, seemed to fail. I finally reached a point of no return. I realized that he was not listening and he was ignoring everything I was trying to say. So eventually after trying to get his attention, I stopped trying. In any event, I finally asked him if he was ready for me to take him home and he just looked at me and walked to the car without saying one word. I wanted to say something, but I did not know what to say. However, my tears were speaking loud and clear. How could this happen? Where was the Harvey that I once knew and what caused him to start snorting cocaine? How could this happen in the short time after I left him?

As I was driving him back home, thoughts ran through my mind and it was hard to stop them. It was so quiet in the car but my tears were speaking loud and clear. At this time in my life I was still not saved and I did not know the Lord.

My tears were pouring from my eyes, almost preventing me from seeing where I was going.

I dropped him off to his mom's house and he opened the door and got out of the car and I ran up to him and hugged him and took his face in my hands and I said to him, "Harvey, I still love you and I always will." He looked at me and I looked at him and I saw in his eyes how much he wanted to be with me yet he couldn't because he loved the drugs more. He walked away and never looked back. This was the last time I saw him.

Although I did not know God at this time, I believe that He protected me once again. I could have agreed to do the drugs with him because I loved him, but something inside of me would not let me do it. I know now that it was God!! I believed that God was using this situation to show me how I was trying to save Harvey's life in the same way that He was trying to save mine. Harvey did not listen to me and I was not listening to Him either. What an unfortunate dilemma!!!

It was His love for me reaching out and protecting me from the love of my life. Harvey was God's creation and God loved him too.

EVEN BEFORE I KNEW HIM, HE PROTECTED ME AND PROTECTED THE ANOINTING INSIDE OF ME!

A GOD ENCOUNTER

Eventually I met and married Kevin after living with him for two years. When I married Kevin, He took real good care of me. He treated me special but I do not know if I loved him and I do not know if he loved me. I guess it was basically a marriage of hope and a marriage of security and convenience. However, I do know if I had love for him, it was not a romantic love but instead, I believe it was a love that you would have for a brother or for a best friend. In retrospect, I also believe that he felt the same about me. In any case, I felt close to him and we were married and I felt a sense of security. I thought this would fill the void that was within me, but little did I know, I was sooo wrong. We got married in 1994. Neither one of us was saved at the time.

When we got married his family did not approve of me and Kevin said it was because I was black. Kevin's mother had told him that in the Bible, it said that sheep and goats do not go together and I was a goat (black) and they were sheep (white). Even though I did not really know God back then, I knew in my heart that was not in the Bible. They did not want any contact with me at all, but it was alright for Kevin to come and visit them. However, Kevin decided to tell them that if I was not invited he would not come either. So for a while we had no contact with them. Maybe Kevin called them once in a while, but we did not go over to their home because they did not want any part of me because I was black. Although His family did not approve of me, based on what Kevin said, His father was more against me than the rest. Kevin and his father were close and I hated to cause conflict between them. They used to go fishing together and did other things together. I felt so bad and even though I was not saved, I began to pray and I asked God to make things right between Kevin and his family but especially Kevin and his dad. I prayed so hard one day that my tears would not stop coming. I asked God to restore this family and make it better than before.

As time passed, Kevin's father had a heart attack and he was taken to the hospital. Kevin's mom called him and asked him to come to the hospital but she told him, do not bring me. Kevin rushed to the hospital to see his dad. In time, Kevin's dad was able to go home and I believe in that same week while he was at home, he had another heart attack. He once again was rushed to the hospital to have a triple-bypass surgery once again. Kevin's mom called Kevin to have him come to the hospital without bringing me. I asked Kevin if I could go with him and he said his mom said no, so I was not allowed to go with Kevin. Meanwhile he left and went to the hospital and I got down on my knees and prayed that his dad would be alright. I prayed that God would be with him and guide the surgeon's hand. Later that day Kevin came home and I could see that he was concerned. I told Kevin that his dad would be alright because I prayed. Sometime later after Kevin's dad came home, he had another heart attack. He was immediately taken back to the hospital. In any event, this time it was different. If I remember correctly, this time his dad called and he asked Kevin to bring me. Kevin could not believe what he heard. As we walked into the hospital and into Kevin's dad's room, I was feeling nervous because I knew that none of them (his family) liked me so I felt like I was walking into a lion's den. As Kevin and I walked into his room, I was walking behind Kevin and most of the family were there.

Without a beat his dad said, "Ann, where are you? Do not walk behind my son, walk beside him."

When Kevin's father said this, the whole family was basically in shock! No one said anything. You could hear a pin drop it was so quiet. I believe that Kevin's father's hardened heart was softened toward me from that day forward. However, I do not believe that God caused the heart attack but it was allowed.

In Proverbs chapter 21: 1-(NIV) it says—"The king's heart is in the hand of the Lord; he directs it like a watercourse wherever he pleases."

I believe that God turned his heart and humbled him and caused him to realize that God loved me and I was His anointed. I do believe that he had an encounter with God. After Kevin's father's encounter with God, He was never the same.

A GOD ENCOUNTER

I do not remember exactly when it happened but after Kevin's dad's heart attacks, my husband and I were invited over to their home for dinners and holidays and birthdays. After the heart attacks, Kevin and His family was close again.

Although my husband and I were able to be a part of the family, and they all went out of their way to treat me nice, I felt the only real, sincere and genuine person was Kevin's dad. Why? Because Kevin's dad was the only one that had an encounter with God and it was real, genuine and authentic.

At this time I was not saved but as you can see, God answered my prayer. After this incident, I would continue to pray to God almost every day and although I was not saved yet, He would still answer my prayers! What a great God!! I called to God and Grace answered me. God said, 'Touch not my anointed!'

TEARS OF DEEP SADNESS

In any event, years after I married Kevin, one afternoon I received a call from my sister, Freda, and she said that she read in the paper that Harvey (My ex-boyfriend) had died. I am not sure what caused his death. When I heard this news it hit me like a tidal wave and suddenly I could not hold back my emotion and the tears flowed from my eyes and I cried and cried. It was like when I heard this news, a part of me died also. It was almost too much for me to handle! I knew that I still had love for him but I did not know just how much. I remember Freda was trying to stop me from crying because she said that I would be hurting my husband's (Kevin) feelings crying over the death of my ex-boyfriend's death. However, I continued to cry and I could not stop. Finally, I told Freda that my husband would understand, but little did I know Freda was one hundred per cent accurate. When I hung up the phone, I shared with Kevin about the death of my ex-boyfriend and he was devastated that my emotion was that strong. He proceeded to ask me to go upstairs out of his sight if I was going to continue to cry over spilled milk. I guess I was wrong expecting my husband to understand what I was going through. You have to realize that Kevin is very sensitive and easily hurt. I could not understand why he did not comfort me in this but it was very hard for him to see me crying over another man even if the other man was not alive. I guess I just did not understand it but

I accepted it. I believe that even though Harvey had died, Kevin still felt threatened by him.

KEVIN WAS DEVASTATED THAT I REACTED SO STRONGLY OVER HARVEY'S DEATH SO I SUFFERED AND MOURNED IN SILENCE.

PLAGUE OF FLIES

At one point in my life, when I was with Harvey, I did not have many dreams or visions. I did not hear much from God after the age of 40.

However, years after I married Kevin, the dreams came back in full force.

I remember one morning waking up and seeing huge black flies covering our ceiling. Although it was not a dream, it was more like a nightmare—it seemed like there were hundreds of these flies. I ran out to the barn to get Kevin and immediately he came upstairs to our bedroom and he did not seem upset or surprised. He got the floor vacuum and vacuumed them up and immediately, they were back again. It was almost like a plague. The more he vacuumed, the faster they came back. He could not keep up!!

It was like a nightmare but I was awake. I had never seen anything like it before. I was speechless. I was frozen and I did not know what to do. All I could think about was to run away from this nightmare. Kevin was working as hard as he knew how, but to no avail. I did not know this at the time but in the Bible, when God told Moses to go and say to Pharaoh, 'let my people go,' Pharaoh did not agree so God sent plagues on Egypt. I was thinking in my head, could it be a slight possibility that God sent these plagues to let me

PLAGUE OF FLIES

know that I was in huge disobedience. Exodus 8: 1-2 NIV New International Version

1Then the Lord said to Moses, "Go to Pharaoh and say to him, 'this is what the Lord says: Let my people go, so that they may worship me. **2**If you refuse to let them go, I will send a plague of frogs on your whole country

Could these flies be a message of judgment? I had many questions but no answers. Nevertheless, I knew that God was against me marrying Kevin but I married him anyway. However, I did not believe that He wanted me to just leave. I continued to have many questions racing in my head. In any event, after hours of hard work, the flies finally let up. I looked at Kevin and I asked him, 'what was that?'

The next day when Kevin was at work, I was fixing me something to eat and I had to go upstairs to get something and right away I noticed the flies were back. Immediately I grabbed the floor vacuum and vacuumed them up and this time I was not shocked, amazed or baffled; but I had a job to do and I did not let up. I was fighting for my life as if my life depended on it and in some ways, I believed that it did. I had a purpose and my purpose was to conquer and win. Although the flies kept coming, I did not give up. I pressed on and persevered and I did not let up and, eventually, they were gone!! Kevin called me from work and asked me how everything was going and I told him that I had another incident with the flies and again, he was not surprised. I guess you have to know Kevin to really get the picture. He is almost never surprised about anything. Usually nothing took him by surprise but there are a few exceptions. In any event, when I got off the phone, I fell to my knees and I asked God to help me. I told God that I wanted to know my mother's God and I asked Him to reveal Himself to me. I told God that I was sooo sorry that all these many years I had been nothing but a pain to Him and I wanted to say that I am sorry. I asked Him to forgive me for being such a huge disappointment to Him. I told Him that I loved Him and I asked Him to forgive me for being an absolute idiot. I told my God that He has been so kind to me, kinder than I deserve. I kept crying because I felt His love and comfort. I felt like He was saying to me,

"Ann, the same way I feel about my son Jesus, I feel about you. You are a Pearl of a great Price and I will fight for you as long as it is necessary. I love you, Ann, and all I want is you and your heart." The tears poured out of my eyes, not drips, but showers that turned into floods. I cried so much that I could not see. I felt so ashamed of how I had treated the one who wanted nothing but the best for me.

I treated Him with no reverence at all and still in my sin, He loved me.

I also told him that I disobeyed Him when he told me not to marry Kevin and I married him anyway. I told God that I was so sorry and I once again asked Him to forgive me. I believe that the Lord said-

ANN, I WANT YOU, I WANT YOUR HEART! Hosea 6:6 New Living Translation (NLT)
⁶ I want you to show love,[a]
not offer sacrifices.
I want you to know me[b]
more than I want burnt offerings.

I do have a confession to make. Before I married Kevin, I believe that He (God) told me not to marry Kevin and I did not obey. You see what kind of person I was. I was totally in disobedience to God and I was not even afraid. However, I did not really know God at the time, but I should have known better, seeing that God had revealed Himself to me so many times. To say the least, I really had no excuse other than the fact that I did not know what I needed to do to be saved. I was rebellious and arrogant and paid no attention to what He said or did. He revealed Himself to me so many times and he has extended nothing but mercy and grace to me. He has covered my failings more times than I can remember. I can say without hesitation that God is love. He does not do love, He is love and I know one thing and that is He really loves me! As I am writing at this very moment, I can't stop crying because I owe Him so much and no one, absolutely no one, knows just how much but Him and me!

His love endures forever. His love is unfailing and divine.

My father, God, heard my prayer and the flies left and they never came back! What an amazing God!

But still, I was not saved

PRAYER OF SALVATION

I prayed a prayer to God and not long after I prayed this prayer, I was watching TCT (a Christian television channel) and one of the ministers led me to the Lord. I did not know there was such a thing.

After I prayed that prayer, I had such a peace that passed all understanding. If God had been standing in front of me, there would not have been a bigger impact.

After these words that I prayed, I knew beyond the shadow of a doubt, that I was saved! I paused for a moment, slowly, cautiously and carefully deliberating every word.

And these words hit me all at once, like a tidal wave and it settled down into my whole being. Suddenly it came to me that I was a real child of the King! How awesome is that! I wanted so much to tell somebody that I just became the child of a King! My heart was pounding and I could not think straight and yet I was torn between two responses—I wanted to share this experience with my husband, Kevin, and yet, I knew He would not understand. So I finally decided to tell him, whether he understood it or not. I kept saying to myself that I was at this time the happiest lady in this whole world and I felt changed somehow! I realized that God is more real than this world.

PRAYER OF SALVATION

I used to feel like a pelican in the wilderness, an owl of the desert and a sparrow alone on the roof top, unfulfilled and rejected and abandoned like an alien in an unknown land. However, I thought Kevin would fill this void, but I was wrong. Then I asked the Lord to come into my heart and the Holy Spirit came into my heart and my life instantly changed. His love captivated my heart and lifted me from the pit of hell and brought me to a place of love. His love felt so real and authentic and sincere and genuine and no fakeness nor phoniness but He was righteous, devoted, faithful and holy and just and He never goes back on His word. I can say without a shadow of doubt that I have never met a man who did not go back on their word, until I met the Lord. I thought to myself,

"NO ONE ON EARTH IS LIKE YOU, AND YOU HAVE NO EQUAL.

IF I THOUGHT I WAS IN LOVE BEFORE, I WAS GREATLY DECEIVED!!"

After I prayed the prayer of salvation, I got down on my knees and I cried for hours because I thought of all the times He tried to get me to come to Him. He went after me with a passion and He did not ever give up. I realized that same day that freedom had come and His love finally found a way to my heart.

I PRAYED TO HIM LIKE I NEVER PRAYED BEFORE. IT WAS A PRAYER FROM MY HEART. I ASKED GOD TO

OVERWHELM MY HEART WITH HIS LOVE, POWER AND PASSION AND MERCY AND TRUTH. I ASKED HIM TO FILL ME UP TO THE POINT THAT I CANNOT EVEN STAND IT. I ASKED HIM TO TEACH ME HOW TO FOLLOW HIM AND TRUST HIM AND I ASKED HIM TO TAKE ME TO A DIMENSION OF INTIMACY THAT I DO NOT EVEN KNOW. I ASKED HIM TO HELP ME TO RELEASE THOSE HIDDEN HURTS SUCH AS UNFORGIVENESS AND BITTERNESS, ARROGANCE AND PRIDE AND REJECTION. I ASKED HIM TO OVER-RIDE ALL MY UNBELIEF AND REPLACE IT WITH HIS TRUTH.

"I STAND IN AWE OF YOU AND YOU GO AHEAD OF ME AND YOU PREPARE A PLACE FOR ME. THANK YOU JESUS!!

"MY SOUL MAGNIFIES THE LORD, AND MY SPIRIT HAS REJOICED IN GOD MY SAVIOR, FOR HE HAS REGARDED THE LOWLY STATE OF HIS MAIDSERVANT, FOR BEHOLD, HENCEFORTH ALL GENERATIONS WILL CALL ME BLESSED, FOR HE WHO IS MIGHTY HAS DONE GREAT THINGS FOR ME AND HIS NAME IS HOLY, HOLY IS HIS NAME."

FATHER GOD, YOU MERELY SPOKE AND THE HEAVENS WERE CREATED, YOU BREATHE A WORD, AND THE STARS WERE BORN. YOU ASSEMBLE THE SEAS IN THEIR BOUNDARIES AND YOU LOCKED IN THE OCEAN AND THE OCEAN STOOD STILL. LORD, I WILL PROCLAIM YOU TO MY BROTHERS AND SISTERS AND I WILL

PRAISE YOUR NAME FOREVER. I WILL ALWAYS PUT MY TRUST IN YOU AND YOU ALONE. I WILL NOT PUT MY TRUST IN POWERFUL PEOPLE BECAUSE THEY WILL DIE AND CARRY THEIR PLANS WITH THEM. I WILL PUT MY TRUST IN YOU!!! YOU ARE AN AWESOME GOD AND YOU ARE THE ONLY GOD AND THERE IS NONE LIKE YOU.

He responded quickly to me: I wrote it while He was speaking. It was like listening prayer! Revelation 3:8-(NIV) Psalm 116:6-(NLT)-Isaiah 66:12-(NIV)

"Ann, I know all the things that you do, and I have opened a door for you that no one can close. You have little strength and yet you obeyed my word and did not deny me. I will protect you for you have childlike faith. I will give you a river of peace and prosperity and the wealth of the nations will flow to you."

God said this to me twice, once before I was saved and now once again when I first received salvation and this is His word that I believe He gave to me.

"Because the people are talking like this, my message will flame out of your mouth and burn the people like kindling wood."

He had given me this word twice and I had been meditating on it and I knew my God would bring it to pass in my life. I was kind of afraid, but He said that He would help

TOUCH NOT MY ANOINTED

me. Once again I believed that He was speaking into my future.

I remember when Kevin came home from work, I could not wait to lead him to my Lord. I told him what had happened and he looked at me and asked me what channel had I been watching? He did not like what I was saying to Him and he said he did not want to hear any more of it. I wanted to share this beautiful good news with my husband and he rejected it. I realized that he reminded me of myself when God tried to get me to come to him and I continued to reject Him. I did not know what to do next. I could not judge Kevin, for I was disobedient for such a long time; but I continued to pray for my husband and I knew that he would eventually be saved. I knew it in my heart!!! I remember reading the Bible and it said that my household will be saved and Kevin was in my household Acts 16:31- (NIV).

After Kevin went to work I prayed to God to put someone in Kevin's path that would lead Kevin to Him. As time went by, whatever I prayed for God answered me. Before I married Kevin, I was diagnosed with lupus and I was in so much pain. I always felt like I had the flu. I had headaches and joint pain and I used to use a walking stick so I would not fall. My hands were in so much pain that I could not pull up my pants. I was on 13-15 different medications. However after I asked Jesus to come in my life, I began to pray to God for Him to make me better and I asked Him to take me off all this medication and God answered my prayer. Praise Jesus!!! The pain left! I no longer felt like I had the flu and I could walk without the cane! I believe that I am healed!

MIRACLES, SIGNS, AND WONDERS

Kevin and I lived on a farm and we had some animals. We had dogs and cats and a lot of sheep. We had the same breed of sheep and they all were the same color. They all looked identical.

One Saturday morning Kevin woke me up and asked me to come with him to Michigan State University to see the baby lambs. It was the season for them to be born. I was so excited to go to see them. When we arrived there, I went into this big building where there were lots of ewes. They had birthed lambs and I picked up a beautiful black one and brown ones. They were all different colors. I was like a kid in a candy store. I picked up a black one because all ours were gray with a black face. I looked at Kevin and I said that I wanted a black one or a brown one and he said it would not be possible because of a genetic code. Kevin said that because we have the same rams and the same kind of ewes, they are going to look the same, unless we could pay for a different breed of a ram and we could have a different color lamb. I looked at Kevin and I looked at the lamb in my hand and told Kevin that I was going to pray to God for a chocolate lamb and he just laughed. Although he laughed, I prayed and I expected that I would get my chocolate lamb. In any event, we got in the car and went home.

MIRACLES, SIGNS, AND WONDERS

In the meantime, our ewes were already pregnant. I believe it was a month or a couple of months later, Kevin went into the barn and saw that the lambs were already birthed. Kevin ran into the house and he said, "Ann, you have to come out here; there is something you have to see."

I said, "Wait until I get dressed. He proceeded to tell me, "We're in the country. Who is going to see you?" I threw on a house coat and went directly to the barn. He led me to the last stable and he asked me to look to the left of the stable and I did. Lo and behold, I saw a baby lamb. Actually, I saw twin lambs.

They looked as if they were just born. The ewe had twins, one was the same color as our other ones, but the other one was a chocolate lamb! I fell to my knees and I thanked God for my lamb that he gave me. I picked him up and hugged him so tight and Kevin was still in shock. His mouth was open and he could not believe what he had seen. He could not believe it! If you know Kevin, he is normally the type of person who is not easily surprised. He is not easily shocked. However, he looked at me with fear in his eyes, making no attempt to hide his sarcasm.

He gazed at me and fell to his knees with tears in his eyes and asked me with his voice intense with anxiety,

"What did I marry? "

This baby lamb scared him, but I seemed to have scared

◄ TOUCH NOT MY ANOINTED

him even more. Kevin could not understand God's miracle because he never seen or experienced miracles before in his life, until now. He thought this was strange, weird, or far out! On the other hand, I knew that this was an answered prayer. I prayed for a chocolate lamb and God answered my prayer because I believed!

Read Matthew 21:22—Mark 11:24.

However, I took the chocolate lamb into my arms and took him into the house. I named him "Chocolate Boy." He became my pet and I loved him. If you would ask why I wanted a black lamb or a chocolate one, it was not really a mystery to me why I prayed for a chocolate lamb! I just wanted one!!!

My life was filled with miracles, signs, and wonders. Every day when I prayed, God would move. He answered all of my prayers.

I remember one day I was looking at TCT. Benny Hinn was on TV and Kevin knew that I was not thrilled with Benny Hinn. As I was watching his show, I heard a voice inside of me that said for me to go and see him. I heard him so clear. I said, "Lord, I do not believe in Benny Hinn," and His voice said, "I DO" His voice also said for me to go and see him and I convinced Kevin to take me to Joe Louis Arena in Detroit. In any event, we went to Joe Louis Arena in Detroit to see Benny Hinn. I walked up to an usher and told him that God Himself asked me to come here to see Benny

MIRACLES, SIGNS, AND WONDERS

Hinn. So therefore, we would like a seat up front. The usher said that people stayed overnight to get a good seat and they are in the balcony. He said you come here at the last minute and you expect to get a seat up front? I looked at him and did not smile and my voice was tense with anxiety and I asked him one question and it was this—

"DID GOD TELL THEM TO COME?" I LOOKED AT HIM AND SAID

"GOD TOLD ME TO COME AND THAT IS WHY WE ARE HERE."

The usher looked at me like he thought I was from Mars. He made no attempt to hide his anger and frustration. He proceeded to point way up in the balcony and told me the only seat that was available was way up there. I then looked at him and said, "God would not tell me to come here to see Benny Hinn on a monitor, he would want me to see him up close and in person."

The usher looked aggravated and his tone was tense and full of sarcasm. He pointed for me to go and we finally climbed the balcony and found a seat. I knew that God wanted me to be up close and personal with him. Nevertheless, we found a seat and sat down. I looked at Kevin and I prayed, "Lord, let your will be done."

Immediately, the minute I prayed that prayer, the same usher was climbing the stairs and Kevin recognized that

◄ TOUCH NOT MY ANOINTED

he was looking at us. All of a sudden the usher pointed for Kevin and me to come and we got up and followed him down to the first floor and he went up to the front and asked the usher to find us a seat up front and we were able to sit in the third row from the front.

I looked at Kevin and I said, "Look what God did!!" Kevin looked at me and once again he was in shock!

When Kevin and I were married, God did so many miracles in our lives through prayer, and yet Kevin kept hardening his heart. Again, he reminded me of myself!! It seemed that the more miracles God performed in our lives, the more Kevin turned against me. However, I continued to pray for Kevin. I was also stubborn and rebellious before I came to the Lord, so therefore, I understood where Kevin was and what he was going through.

In any case, as we were sitting up front at Joe Louis Arena, Benny Hinn asked the sick to walk on the stage and I had back pain and I begged Kevin to go to the podium with me but to no avail. All of a sudden, Benny said, "If you are not able to come up, Be Healed." I looked at Kevin and I told him I had no more back pain! I was healed!!! Blind people were able to see and the crippled left their wheelchairs and got up and walked. God let me see that Benny Hinn was His and I then believed!!! I knew that day that Benny was real and genuine and authentic. God wanted me to know that.

It meant a lot to (God) for me to know that Benny Hinn was His!!!

My beautiful Lord, my beautiful Savior and my best friend.

God was moving in my life with His presence, miracles, signs and wonders.

THE EPITOME OF EVIL

I would like to reiterate, at one point in my life the dreams stopped from God, but when I married Kevin, the dreams returned. I would like to share another dream and this dream scared me. It was so real, as if it was actually happening. However, I had no idea what was about to happen! I had no idea what was coming next, but I knew that this dream was a vision of our future, and I did not know what to do to stop it.

In this dream, I was sitting at the kitchen table and all of a sudden, I saw this huge snake. It was sitting right beside me and in this dream I froze and I could not speak. I was so afraid and then I woke up. My heart was pounding and I could not think straight and I could not compute it in my head what this dream meant. I screamed and told Kevin that Satan was trying to divide and conquer our marriage. I felt like God had given me some interpretation, but it was not real clear. Somehow I felt that Satan was going to try to turn Kevin against me and I believed that God gave me that revelation, although I had some reservations. I warned Kevin that something was going to happen, because these dreams that I normally have are prophetic. Kevin looked at me and just walked away. He did not believe anything that I was saying to him. Kevin did not have a clue what was about to happen. He did not have any idea what was coming. Days went by and even weeks, and all I could think about was this dream. It was almost impossible for me to sleep. I was torn between two impulses. I was not sure whether I should tell someone or just keep it only between me and Kevin.

Remember when the serpent spoke to Eve in the garden. The serpent was more cunning than any beast of the field which the Lord God had made. And the serpent said to the woman "has God indeed said, you shall not eat of every tree of garden?" And the woman said to the serpent, "We may eat the fruit of the tree of the garden. But the fruit of the tree which is in the midst of the garden, God has said, you shall not eat it, nor shall you touch it, lest you die." And the serpent said "you should surely not die, for God knows in that day you will be like God knowing good and evil. And the woman saw that the fruit was pleasant to the eyes and the woman did eat." You see the enemy came in and spoke to Eve and caused her to disobey.

Read Genesis, Chapter 3

I believe that Satan was going to speak to Kevin and I tried to give Kevin a warning, but he did not take heed. The enemy was going to try to divide and conquer our marriage. Satan is cunning, subtle, and crafty. The enemy comes to steal and kill and destroy and that is his purpose. God comes so we can have life and have it more abundantly. John 10:10-(NKJV)—**The thief** does not **come** except to **steal**, and to **kill**, and to **destroy**. I have **come** that they may have life, and that they may have it more abundantly.

TOUCH NOT MY ANOINTED

I believe that God gave me that dream so Kevin and I could pray against the plans of the enemy. I began to pray diligently against the enemy's plans. However, Satan baited a trap and Kevin fell right into it. Kevin had no clue!

I told Kevin that evil was lurking at our door and we needed to pray. He did not listen. Later, I saw a huge change in my husband's personality. He was not himself. He was totally like a different person and immediately I connected it to the dream.

One day I was in the kitchen and Kevin looked at me in a look that was not him. It was a look from another source and I saw it. It was almost like Kevin was possessed. He changed into a whole different person and I prayed for God to help him and me. Weeks after I had dreams, our animals began to die, one right after another. The whole thing did not seem real! We had about 30 sheep and tons of cats and a couple of dogs. I remember several of our ewes abandoned their babies (lambs) and I immediately went to Tractor Supply Store and bought some powdered milk designed for lambs and I tried to feed them myself with a bottle and this powder milk for lambs when their mother dies in childbirth. However not one of these babies survived. In the meantime, the babies were dying like flies but my chocolate lamb survived. Not only did he survive but he thrived. He was one of few that lived! He was very healthy and whole! I remember feeding many of these babies from a bottle for about three or four weeks and in the fifth week, I went out to feed them, they were dead.

THE EPITOME OF EVIL

This happened more times than you can imagine. I cried a whole lot. Every time a lamb died, a part of me died too. Seeing how I would go out and feed them three or four times a day, they felt like my babies, since I had never had children of my own. I also remember bottle feeding one newborn and after three days, I noticed that she was not breathing and I kept feeding her anyway because I did not want to accept the death of another one of our lambs and Kevin came over to me and told me to stop because the lamb had died. I kept feeding it because I wanted to make her come back to life. However, it did not happen. In any event, not only did our lambs die but some of our cats died and many of them just vanished without a trace. I remember one time in particular we had a snow white kitten. This kitten was not very friendly. When you fed her, she would hiss at you. All you needed to do was just look at her the wrong way and she would get angry. One day I noticed that she was acting unusual. She was not the cranky cat like before so I mentioned it to Kevin and he went and picked her up and he noticed there was a big hole in her forehead. I do not remember exactly what he did but after he did it, worms began to crawl out of her head, one after another. It was like a horror movie. I do not want to sound eerie but we counted about ten worms that came from her head and the next day, she disappeared and we never saw her again. Eerie things continued to happen after I had that dream of the huge black snake. I knew in my heart that it was a prophetic dream from God warning me of evil to come and it came with a vengeance! This dream was not a mystery, but it was a message replaying itself in real life.

In the last years of our marriage, it was basically no marriage at all. We had no intimacy and no relationship. I hardly saw Kevin because he was either at work or working on the farm or spending time with his girlfriend. The Kevin that I married was no longer around. He changed so much. It was like I was living with a stranger. I would sit under the tree waiting for him to come home and when he did come home, he would not talk. I could see that he was so unhappy and I wanted to do something to help us but no matter what I did, it did not work. One day I decided to clean out his truck and I found a Playboy magazine under his seat. This was so out of his character. He would have never done something like that before.

I knew that the enemy was already trying to steal and kill and destroy our marriage and I prayed to God for Satan to get out of our lives but it seemed that Kevin was a puppet and Satan was pulling his strings. It was almost as if my husband, Kevin, had died and another person was raised up. I did not know him anymore nor did I want to. I was basically a new convert so I did not know how to pinpoint my prayers.

One day Kevin was on the computer and I passed by the computer and I realized that he was on the computer talking with his girlfriend. I was so hurt, actually, I was devastated! I asked myself how I could have given my life to be with someone so cruel. It was at the time almost too horrible for me to acknowledge that he was betraying me with another woman.

I asked him how could he do that to me and he looked at me, making no attempt to hide his anger! If looks could kill, I would have been dead. His voiced was raised, tense with anxiety and almost shaking. However, I will not repeat what he said to me. In any event, I began to cry, for I knew that it was not Kevin. I believe that it was a spirit controlling him.

One day he and I were in the living room and he was crying and I asked him why was he crying and he said that he did not know for sure what he wanted. I told him that I knew one thing and that was, he did not want me anymore. I felt so sorry for him because he was being controlled by the enemy and he did not even know it. I believe the enemy had put in his life a woman with enticing speech, flattering lips and a crafty heart. She seduced him with her words like the snake in the garden that seduced Eve. It was like he was torn between two impulses—the urge to be the Kevin that I once knew and the urge to be controlled by the evil spirit who was controlling the seductress! He was in dire need of spiritual warfare and I did not know at that time how to help him.

I do not want people to think that it was all Kevin's fault. I spent a lot of time braiding my hair and sometimes I was not there for him. Once I became born again, I spent quite a lot of time studying and I loved it and I wanted so much for us to study together but Kevin just did not want any part of the Bible or me. However, my neighbor and I began to have Bible studies and I enjoyed them tremendously. Her

TOUCH NOT MY ANOINTED

name is Wendy. I do not know what I would have done without my God and my neighbor. I believe that God arranged for our divine connection and our strategic alliance.

As time went on, I saw less and less of Kevin. At one point, he would go to the beer tent in Williamston and he would not come back home until early morning. I guess that he was out with his girlfriend (the seductress).

Although in the beginning, I really did not understand the feelings that I had for Kevin, I admired him and I was determined to make our marriage work. However I did not admire the person who he became. It was almost like someone came and took over his body and mind and left a stranger. Sometimes, I did not even feel comfortable with him. I would look at him and I would see different eyes from Kevin looking back at me. I prayed and prayed and asked God to deliver me from this hell. I know without a shadow of a doubt that God protected me. I could have died like all of those animals. I could have gone insane, but God showed up and protected me and saved my life.

Nothing was going to touch His anointed!

It was not really a good life because it was full of burdens and strongholds. I did not feel like I was living, I sometimes felt like I was the walking dead. I felt trapped and I did not know what to do. As time passed, Kevin asked me if I wanted to leave and I felt like he wanted me to but I did not really want to go. Finally, I just left and moved out anyway and it was the best decision I ever made.

Although I missed the Kevin I once knew, I also felt that he was no longer living but the enemy had raised up a replacement—someone who hated me!

A WORD FROM GOD

One day as I was driving down the expressway, I believe that God spoke clearly to me. He asked me to go to my husband's job and read Proverbs 5 to him. I pulled off the expressway to read what I believed God wanted me to read to my husband. As I turned the page to read Proverbs 5, I was shocked. I had no idea that this was even in the Bible. The title was "The Peril of Adultery." You have to remember I was basically a new convert and I do not even know at that time if I had ever read the entire Bible. However, I could not do what I thought God had asked me to do because these words sounded like me and I knew Kevin would not listen. In the meantime, I drove back onto the freeway and went straight home. You are not going to believe what happened next! When I arrived home I went into my apartment and turned on a Christian channel, I believe it was channel 19 at this time. There was a pastor preaching and he looked right into the camera and said,

"There is someone who just tuned in who is running from God. God asked you to do something and you are not doing it." He then looked into the camera for a second time and he said once again, "when God asks you to do something, you need to do it now!!"

I was once again in shock. That man was talking to me as if he saw me through the television. I immediately picked up my Bible and drove to Kevin's workplace. I went to his custodial office and asked him if I could come in and he said yes. I told him what I thought God had said to me and he thought it was funny. I knew he would not understand but I did it anyway. I asked him if I could read to him Proverbs 5 (NKJV) and he agreed. After I read it to him, he proceeded to ask me to explain to him what it meant. I told him that God is not pleased with what he was doing. I told him that he was committing adultery and that was a sin to God. By this time Kevin had moved into his home a married woman and they both were committing adultery. I asked him to listen to God and be obedient or there would be some serious consequences. He looked at me and began to laugh. He did not take seriously what God had spoken to him. I could see that Kevin was in defiance and rebelling against God's Word.

I LOOKED AT HIM AND TEARS BEGAN TO FLOW DOWN MY FACE. I WAS CRYING NOT BECAUSE I WAS HURTING FOR ME, BUT I WAS HURTING FOR HIM.

I knew God was trying to give him a second chance and Kevin did not take it. I believe God did not want us to get married at first, but since we did, I believe that God honored this marriage. I told Kevin that he was going to reap the fruit of his own ways and he would be caught in the traps of his own schemes, if he did not obey God's Word.

However, he continued to laugh at God and at me. He once again looked at me and said, "Ann, you see why we are not together? You are strange!"

TOUCH NOT MY ANOINTED

I continued to cry because he did not know what he was doing. I then stopped crying and I looked at him and he looked at me and I saw from his eyes a look of sadness. I hugged him and turned to run out of his office and he held me and asked me not to leave, but he wanted me to wait until I stopped crying. I pulled away from him and left his office and before I left the building, I said, "God, I shake the dust off my feet and I leave him to his own fate." I do not know where those words came from. It was as if the Holy Spirit spoke through me.

I do not remember much after this except when he called back two weeks later. When he called, he was crying. He said, "I have to tell you what I have been going through." He had accidents with both of his trucks and he had to get a ride to work with his neighbor. The first accident, a deer ran out in front of his new truck and it was badly damaged so he put it in the shop and the following day, he drove his other truck to work and on the way home, he skidded off the road and now he had no other way of transportation. In the meantime, his girlfriend owned a horse and one day she got on the horse and it threw her and now she was in the hospital all bruised up and in a lot of pain. Also, his girlfriend's children were taking from her and she lost her job. He kept telling me all these things that were happening and he did not understand them. He also said that the city had come out and looked over his property and they told him that he needed to clean up his place and if he did not, he would be fined every day until he cleaned up his yard and field. He said that all those many years you and

I were together, the city did not complain once and now that you are not here, they are complaining. He said that he did not understand. He said his girlfriend said that it was all

Ann's fault. She told Kevin that I had put a curse on them. However, Kevin said that he defended me. He told her that

Ann would never do anything wicked like that. He proceeded to tell her (his girlfriend) how wrong she was. Kevin told me that he went out of his way to defend me because he knew that I was not that kind of person!

He said that if Ann was praying, she was praying God's will be done.

HANDPRINT OF THE ENEMY

Weeks later, Kevin called me to ask me if I could come and visit him before the divorce was final. I asked him was this lady still living there with him and he said, "Yes, but if you say the right thing, we can move her out and move you back in." He then asked me to come when she was at work and I reluctantly agreed. The next day, I went to his home and she was not there. Kevin said that he had a proposition for me. I asked him to say it.

Beloved, you are not going to believe what he asked me to do.

It was almost like listening to Harvey when he came to Okemos and he wanted me to snort the cocaine with him. It was for sure the handprint of the enemy replaying itself once again.

Kevin said that he wanted me to be the person that he married. He said that when I got saved, I really changed. He said if I would be the person that he married and it would be just him and me without God, and if I agreed to that, he would move this lady out of the house and I could help him and he would move me back in. I looked at him and repeated what I thought he said, I said, "Let me get this straight. You want me to give up the only One in my life that really loved me. The only One in my life who took me in and loved me and comforted me and encouraged me and was relentlessly kind to me when you found someone else that you loved, and you wanted to be with her and not me. You want me to give up my very best friend, my savior and my Lord and my Father? You want me to give Him up for you? Is this correct?"

And he said yes and I said, "I would rather die first than to give up my God for you or for anyone." I told Kevin that I did still love him as a friend, but I loved God more than anything. I also told him that the love that I have for him pales compared to the love that I have for my God. I went on to say that God's love is unchanging and unfailing and unconditional. I pleaded with Kevin to get to know God and his life would change for the better. I told Kevin that I would not apologize for making that decision because I knew it was right. Kevin said that he wanted us try again and I said I could not try again on those conditions. We parted ways and the divorce was finalized. When we went to the Courthouse to get divorced, the judge asked us if we indeed wanted this divorce. Kevin was frozen as if he could not speak. The judge then repeated it a second time and Kevin was looking down as though he was having second thoughts. I, on the other hand, spoke up loud and clear. I said, "Yes, we do want to be divorced."

Even today, I miss the Kevin I used to know, the Kevin that took me on long boat rides and trips. I miss the Kevin who would get me up in the middle of the night and we would travel on the spur of the moment, take a short trip out of town! I still sometimes miss how kind he used to be to me. He would buy me anything I wanted but I was not happy! I hardly ever saw him and he was always so busy. He was to me a person that I once really admired! He said that I changed when I asked Jesus into my life but he changed also. I guess we were two different people that were not ever meant to be together. He changed and so did I. However, I changed for the better because I now have the Lord in my life.

Sometime later, after the divorce, Kevin's mom called me to tell me that Kevin was in the hospital and he was asking to see me. I dropped what I was doing and I drove to the hospital and I ran to his bedside and I saw that he was sick. He told me that he was on the tractor and he had fallen on the ground and someone found him and took him to the doctor. I think he said that he was diagnosed with a seizure. I was so glad to see him and I took his hand and held it. Immediately, I was torn between two impulses—I wanted to sit by his side all day and tell him how much I still miss him but at the same time, I wanted to run as fast as I could to put him in my past. However, I began to listen to what he had to say. He did not waste any time but he spoke slowly, cautiously and carefully deliberating every word. His tone was intense and his voice was almost shaking. Instantly he began to explain to me every detail of what happened that caused him to be in the hospital. After he was done talking, I asked him if he would die today, did he know whether he would go to heaven or to hell and he immediately responded with anger. His voice was intense and filled with sarcasm. He told me that he wanted me to come to see him and he did not want me to talk about God.

THE HIGH POINT OF MY LIFE

At least I thought it was.

Consequently, when I went to the hospital, I listened to my former husband talk and after he finished talking, he finally asked me what he needed to do to be saved. My heart was pounding, I could not think straight, and I realized that this was the moment that I had been waiting for since my salvation. I was intrigued and amused all at the same time. I believe that this was one of the happiest days of my life. Instantly, I led him to the Lord!! Praise the Lord!! I mentioned to Kevin that he should find a good church that preaches the Word of God so he could have a church family. I also told him to get into the Word and read it every day to renew his mind. He saw that I was so excited and I wanted him to be excited also. Leading anyone to the Lord is the high point of my life, especially leading Kevin. When you know God as well as I do, you cannot help but share the love of God to every man or woman that you meet. 1 Timothy 2: 1-4-(ESV) English Standard Version:

"First of all, then I urge that supplication, prayers, intercession, and thanksgiving be made for all people, for kings and all who are in high positions that we may lead a peaceful and quiet life, godly and dignified in every way. This is good, and it is pleasing in the sight of God our Lord and Savior, who desires all people to be saved and to come to the knowledge of the truth."

In any event, it is God's will for us to share the Gospel to all men so they can be led to the Lord and to truth (although, I haven't quite done that yet).

I may be wrong, but it seems that some people try to please people, instead of trying to please God, so their heart is not fully committed to God when they ask Jesus to come into their life. I may be wrong again, but I believe that was the case with Kevin. He was trying to please me, not the Lord. I believe that he asked Jesus into his heart for that purpose!

When you ask Jesus into your life God wants you to believe with your heart and say from your mouth that Jesus is Lord and you will be saved. Check out Romans 10:9-(NIV) **9** that if you confess with your mouth, "Jesus is Lord," and believe in your heart that God raised him from the dead, you will be saved.

God wants sincerity!

Hours later after I led my former husband (Kevin) to the Lord, I left and went home. I have seen him several times since that day but I have not seen any fruit. However—I am still praying!! God can do anything, and He is not through with him yet!! God is not through with any of us yet!! I am still in the process of becoming the person that God has called me to be. I am far from perfect. The only perfect person is Jesus. In other words, I will never give up

TOUCH NOT MY ANOINTED

on Kevin because God did not give up on me. Every day, Kevin is in my prayers. God loves him sooo much. I can say one thing about Kevin and that is when he is not under bad influence, he has a kind heart. God is still working and I pray every day that God will chase him down like a wild horse and come up on him and overtake him with great blessings. I believe that Kevin is coming in sooner than he thinks!

TITANIC/AMERICA

UNLESS WE TURN

Titanic/America is heading toward an iceberg

Titanic/ America—An ancient drama replaying itself in a modern world!

UNLESS WE TURN

According to the Wikipedia, the free encyclopedia, The Titanic was a British passenger liner that sank in the North Atlantic Ocean on April 15, 1912 after colliding with an iceberg during her Maiden Voyage from Southampton UK to New York City, US Wikipedia. The Titanic was the largest passenger liner in service at the time. Titanic had an estimated 2,224 people on board when she struck an iceberg. Her sinking two hours and forty minutes later on Monday April 15 resulted in the death of more than 1,500 people, which made it one of the deadliest peacetime maritime disasters in history. Titanic received six warnings of sea ice on April 14, but was traveling near her maximum speed when she sighted the iceberg. Unable to turn quickly enough, the ship suffered a blow that buckled her starboard (right) side and opened five of her sixteen compartments to the sea.

The crew then realized that the ship was going to sink.

They used rocket flares and radios (wireless) messages to attract help, as the passengers were put into life boats. The ship was carrying far too few lifeboats for everyone and many boats were not filled to their capacity due to poorly managed evacuation.

Date..............April 14-15 1912

Time...............23:40-02:20

Location.........North Atlantic Ocean

Cause..............Collision of Iceberg

Outcome..........between 1,490 & 1,635 deaths-

Hear now my words: If there is a prophet among you, I, the Lord, make myself known to him in a vision; I speak to him in a dream Numbers 12:6-(NKJV).

And it shall come to pass afterward that I will pour out My spirit on all flesh; Your sons and your daughters shall prophesy, your old men shall dream dreams, your young men shall see visions. Joel 2:28-(NKJV)

I would like to share something with you that I experienced years ago. It was a terrifying dream but it was so real. To be honest with you, I am not sure if it was a dream or a vision! Nevertheless, I do believe that this dream/vision is definitely a message that holds the key to America's future. At one point God wanted me to pray about it. However, I believe now is the time for this dream/vison to be revealed! This dream's among many that are too critically important to be ignored! Sometimes all that is required is the right time to act and I know that time is now because once again God placed this word in my heart with a burning intensity! Listen to this amazing dream!

One night I decided to lie down on the couch and immediately I fell asleep. Although I thought that I was asleep, it was more like a vision. I had a dream/vision and it seemed so real! It was so vivid and so profound that I literally woke up in tears! My heart was pounding; I was frozen to the point that I could not think straight. I could not process what I felt God was saying to me in this dream. However, I paused for a moment, carefully considering the message behind this frightful dream. As I was meditating, trying to digest it all, a clue came to me the way nothing came to me before. It was an alarm—a warning, a heartbreaking revelation! I realized that God was showing me the future of a modern day drama and it was catastrophic. Later that day, I was lying on the living room floor and all of a sudden, it hit me like a ton of bricks that a voice/thoughts within me was speaking. At one point I almost wanted to dismiss what I thought I was hearing and suddenly the thoughts within me grew louder and these words flooded my spirit.

"Ann, watch and listen. Pay close attention to everything I have shown you in the past and am showing you now.

Ann, I am using this message to prepare their hearts for my return. You have been brought here so I can show you many things. Then you will return to my people and tell them everything you have heard and seen. Ann, it is time for you to bring to remembrance everything that I have shown you and this is the appointed time to proclaim it and put it in writing. Do not be afraid for I am with you and I will help you and I will make all your efforts successful. Always remember that whatever my people go through, let them know that they, too, are not alone!

Suddenly I was led to the verse Isaiah 41:10-(AMP)

"Fear not, (there is nothing to fear), for I am with you; do not look around you in terror and be dismayed, for I am your God. I will strengthen and harden you to difficulties, yes, I will help you; yes, I will hold you up and retain you with my righteous right hand of rightness and justice.

At first the silence was so intense, I was afraid to voice what I thought I heard and the verse that I read. I paused for a moment, cautiously and carefully deliberating every word that was spoken and what was read. My heart was pounding and I could not think straight and I could not process it. Again, I was drawn back, considering every word that was spoken to me and then it hit me all at once that now is the appointed time for God's message to be revealed and His words to be spoken to the world! I realized that the right time is now!! I was torn with two impulses—the urge to run and never look back or the urge to be obedient to the word of God. The whole thing did not seem real. I was once again drawn back to all the things the Lord had shown me when I was a little kid up to now! I did not know where to begin. Suddenly, I heard myself say under my breath, 'I have to do what my God tells me to do, I have to say what I believe my God is telling me to say;' and then it hit me like a ton of bricks. People want to hear what is pleasant and what is an illusion, they do not want to hear the truth. In Isaiah 30:10-(NIV) "They say to the seers, see no more visions, and they say to the prophets, give us no more vision of what is right! Tell us pleasant things and prophesy illusions!"

Nevertheless, I have to please God and not man. I will proclaim to the world what I believe I have seen and what I believe I have heard; and if I perish, I perish!!

When I was a child, I had dreams and visions. Not ordinary dreams and visions, but prophetic ones. It was not unusual for me to have a dream that actually came to pass. If I were to count them, it would be more than the stars in the sky or the sand of the sea. However, my mom did not allow me to share the dreams because many of them could be interpreted as warnings. I think that they frightened her and she wanted me to only tell people encouraging and uplifting pleasant things to give them hope.

Again I repeat. Prophets are not popular, because they speak what is right, not what is popular. It is in the Bible, Isaiah 30:10, NIV. "They say to seers, 'See no more visions!'

and unto the prophets, 'Give us no more visions of what is right! Tell us pleasant things, prophecy illusions. However, I believe that false prophets have arrived and they are performing at this very moment.

I believe with all of my heart that these are the last days and the signs of the times are here, not coming but are already here. 1 Timothy 4:1-New International Version (NIV)

The word clearly says that in latter times some will abandon the faith and follow deceiving spirits and things taught by demons.

I believe that day is here! I believe that all the warnings are clear in the Bible. Recently I was reading a magazine from Dr. Jack Van Impe and he believes as I do that the warnings are clear and they cannot be misunderstood. Look at this excerpt by Dr. Jack Van Impe:

"The warnings are clear, in the pages of Scripture. The Bible's warning in 1 Timothy cannot be misunderstood: In the latter days, ministers will betray the Lord Jesus- Why? They will believe lies. They will be taken in by the delusions and deceptions of apostates, antichrist and super deceivers. They will give heed to "seducing spirits and doctrines of demons" (1 Timothy 4:1). According to Dr. Jack Van Impe, This is no longer "prediction"—this is present day! This is happening now. I agree with him 100% and it is crucial that you should get his video as soon as possible. My husband and I are going to order it online. It is called –Jack Van Impe Prophecy Bible. Visit his web address jvim.com

I have good reason to believe that when God speaks to me in dreams and visions, I can no longer ignore them. Why? Because I truly believe God is using me in these end times along with others to proclaim His messages to the whole world in my writing. Although I have recorded many of them, not one of them have escaped my memory. I realize now that God has chosen me to write and be His mouth piece to the world. Many of the dreams that God has given me are not pleasant but are to be taken as warnings. Some people will hear my messages and will not listen, but others will hear and take heed. I know that most people would prefer encouraging messages to make them feel good, but the messages that I have for the world are not only warnings but they are alarming. These are the last days and God said in His word that He would not bring anything on the world without His prophet proclaiming it. I believe that God is using Dr. Jack Van Impe—and Jonathan Cahn—and Dr. Ben Carson, just to name a few. Yes, and I also believe that He is using me. These are end time events that I believe are coming upon the world! **Take heed—watch and pray.**

Surely the Lord God does nothing, unless He reveals His secret to His servants the prophets. Amos 3:7 — NKJV

Here I am, world, proclaiming the messages that I believe are from God Himself speaking to me in dreams and visions and I am proclaiming it to the world! I believe with

TOUCH NOT MY ANOINTED

all of my heart that I was called into being for the will of God and dedicated to His purposes from conception. God has given me a message and now is the time to proclaim it. It has nothing to do with me but everything to do with Him (Jesus).

Please listen and take heed!!

Years ago I had a dream of a huge ship. This ship was heading downstream. I was not sure of the direction. I will just say that it was heading downstream. It was gigantic! I have never seen anything like it!

As I was gazing at this ship in a distance, I noticed it was heading downstream fast. It was heading the opposite direction from where I was standing. Sometimes I am not sure if it is a dream or a moving vision. Whatever the case may be, this ship was so clear in my mind and it was humongous. All of a sudden, it was as if someone had a camera and had zoomed in on this ship and it was no longer in the distance, it was up close. As I continued to gaze in that direction, I saw something big that was right in its path and this huge ship was heading toward it. I remember in this dream I wanted to call for help but I could not speak and even if I did, no one could hear me. Suddenly, I woke up from this terrifying experience (dream or vision) and a voice within my spirit said-

That ship is the Titanic and it collided with the iceberg and the Titanic sunk!!

TITANIC/AMERICA

I thought to myself, why is God showing me something that happened long ago and what does this mean? Immediately, I believe that God responded to my heart.

The huge ship (Titanic) is America heading down the wrong path and if it does not change direction, America is going to run into that iceberg and America will sink.

All of a sudden, I could not think straight. My heart was pounding. I could not process what I believe God was saying to me. Suddenly, I was torn between two impulses-

The urge to share or to keep it within myself and just pray about it. I believe that I finally got the "go ahead" to share, first with the early morning prayer group and now with the world! I went to my early morning prayer which I lead on Monday morning (about two years ago). After we finished with the worship, I told the prayer group about the dream that I had. Everybody was in agreement that we should cry out to God in urgency and ask Him to give us mercy and grace instead of what we deserve, justice. We prayed fervent prayers for our nation and we asked God to give our leaders wisdom, revelation knowledge and sharp discernment to make decisions according to God's will and not according to their will. We also prayed that this nation will turn to God. God is so merciful and if we pray and turn, I know that God will lift the judgments that are headed our way.

Read 2 Chronicles 7: 14—(NIV) "If my people who are

called by my name, will humble themselves and pray and seek my face and turn from their wicked ways, then I will hear from heaven, and I will forgive their sin and will heal their land."

Read 1 Corinthians 7: 14—(NKJV) "But thanks be to God who gives us victory through our Lord Jesus Christ."

Read 2 Corinthians 2:14-(NKJV) "Thanks be to God who always leads us in triumph in Christ and through us diffuse the fragrance of His knowledge in every place."

Let's consider this next verse in Psalms 127: 1-(NIV)

"Unless the Lord builds the house, the builders labor in vain. Unless the Lord watches over the city, the guards stand watch in vain."

We as a nation have taken prayer and Scriptures out of schools. We have taken God out of our media. We have taken Him out of government. God was driven out of our nation's public life. As we have taken Jesus out, people have replaced Him with greed, idols of food, success, self—worship and self-obsession, movie stars, computers, cellphones etc. We as a nation have abandoned our God of Abraham, Isaac and Jacob with idolatry! We have violated God's laws, twisted His truth and broken His covenant. We literally drove Him out of our nation and when something devastating happens, we ask, where is God? The answer is, we sent Him away! Consequently, if we do not turn back to God, we will eat the fruit of our own ways and will be caught in the traps of our own schemes! In other words, if we do not turn to God, Judgment is coming!

"God said 'when I called, they did not answer, and when I spoke they did not listen. They deliberately sinned right before my eyes and they chose to do what they know I despise'" Isaiah 66:4 (NLT).

He was talking about Israel and now He is talking about America. In these last days , not only have I been sent by God to sound an alarm, warning the nation of the profound ramifications for America's future if we do not turn back to Him, but He has and is sending many of His "unknown men who are hearing from God and proclaiming His message. God is trying so hard to awaken America up from rebellion and if we do not wake up, we will run into the iceberg. It will not be God's fault, but it will be our own. Again I repeat. If we do not listen to the voice of God speaking through His prophets, we will eat the fruit of our own ways and will be caught in the traps of our own schemes.

Let us look at just a few things that our nation is doing.

"When the righteous are in authority, the people rejoice, but when a wicked man rule, the people groan."

The people are groaning!! The whole nation is groaning! Look at 9/11, Crash of Wall Street. Bad Economy, and War in Iraq, just to name a few.

TOUCH NOT MY ANOINTED

1. Same sex Marriage, President of the USA supports. Leviticus 20:13—"If a man also lie with mankind as he lieth with a woman, both of them have committed an abomination."

Romans 7—"That is why God abandoned them to their shameful desires. Even the woman turned against the natural way to have sex and instead indulged in sex with each other, and the men instead of having normal relations with a woman, burned with lust for each other. And as a result of that sin, they suffered within themselves the penalty they deserved.

According to God's Word, He is not pleased with women lying with women and men lying with men. This is an abomination to Him. We need to turn!

2. Abortions (also supported by the President of the United States)

Psalm 139:13—For you formed my inward parts, you covered me in my mother's womb.

Jeremiah 1:5 –Before I formed you in the womb, I knew you; before you were born I sanctified you and ordained you to be a prophet to the nations.

In Psalms and Jeremiah God said that He knew us before we were formed in our mom's womb. This signifies to me that no one was born a mistake. God knew you before you were formed in your mom's womb so he picked out the right parents for you. If God knew you and then He sent you here, He had a plan for you. However, when you kill God's baby that He sent here for His purpose, this says to me, that you destroyed a baby that God orchestrated to be here. You overrode God's plan for your own sake. God does not want any babies to be aborted. In Jeremiah chapter 19:5-(NLT) God says-

"They have built pagan shrines to Baal and there they burn their sons as sacrifice to Baal. I have never commanded such a horrible deed." When we have an abortion, we are our own god and we sacrifice our babies to meet our needs.

God did not plan such a thing. He said that it never even crossed His mind to do such a thing.

However, if you have had one abortion or many abortions, do not feel guilty. We all make mistakes. I made this mistake also when I was younger. I did not speak on this so you would feel guilty. If you have asked Jesus into your life, and since then you have had an abortion, God says that if you confess your sin, He is faithful and just to cleanse you of all unrighteousness (1 John 1:9). He will remember it no more!!

On the other hand, if you had an abortion before you asked Him into your life, that sin has been erased and He said that He will remember it no more!! What a miracle!!

If you are reading this book and you have not asked Jesus into your life, you can do it right now. Just say,

"Jesus, come into my life, forgive me for my sin, be my Lord and be my Savior." If you prayed that prayer and you really meant it in your heart, you are saved and the angels in heaven are having a huge party and your name has been written down in the Lamb's Book of Life and your sins are remembered no more.

Getting back to talking about our nation heading down the wrong path, consider these headlines—

Ten Commandments Taken Down

Nativity Scenes Banned

Prayer Prohibited

Under God Removed from the Pledge

Removing Prayer and Scriptures from the Schools.

Exchanging Spirituality for Sensuality

As you see, in this world, there is so little resemblance of the Garden He first created!

We need to pray for our leaders to get us back on track. What used to be sacred in this nation is no longer called sacred, but it is called outdated and immoral. What used to be considered immoral now is called sacred. Everything has turned upside down in America. No wonder America is heading toward the iceberg. We have rejected the one who made this nation blessed among all nations. No one among all nations has been given so much as we have been given. America became the most powerful, the most prosperous, and the most blessed nation on earth from the very beginning. It was God who chose us like He chose Israel. Israel went down. Why? Because they rejected God and turned from His ways and worshipped other gods. The blessings left and when you are not blessed, you are cursed with a cursed.

America has also turned away from God. It is like the same thing happening all over again, first Israel, and now America.

I have to tell this nation, if we do not turn from this path, there are going to be some devastating results. I have seen other things in my dreams that I do not dare to tell. Please hear my heart. We need to turn back to God not later but right now. The ship (America) is sailing fast toward the iceberg and we can stop the direction in which the ship is heading and we can prevent the sinking of our nation.

President Obama should have the whole nation get down on our knees and pray and ask Jesus to forgive us for our sin; this nation needs to totally turn from our own ways to God's ways. We, as a nation need to repent for abortions, idolatry (whether it is money, food, materialism, any things that you put before God), prayerlessness, hatred, homosexuality, adultery, pornography, pride, gossip, lukewarmness, unforgiveness, rebellion, boastfulness, gluttony, selfishness, lack of affection and many more. We need to repent as a nation and turn to God. We need to repent corporately and we need to repent individually. We need to put Scriptures and prayer back in our schools. We need to put God back in our public life. We need to put the Ten Commandments back into the public view and the public square.

We need to read the Bible and let God's agenda be our agenda and God's priority be our priority. We need to learn to hate what God hates and love what God loves. We also need to ban policies, rules and regulations that violate God's laws.

We need to call what God said is sacred, sacred and we need to call what God said is immoral, immoral.

Look at the ship Titanic. It was the biggest ship and no one believed that it could sink. I heard long ago that men used to say that "even God could not sink the Titanic" and look what happened! It sunk, killing most of the people that were on board. Based on what I read, there were warnings a day before that icebergs were seen in the ocean but apparently the day that they (Titanic) spotted the large iceberg, the ship was going too fast to take a different path. Look at America. We have been given warning from different prophets that if we do not turn back to God, there are going to be devastating results! Are the leaders listening? No, they have hardened their hearts and deafened their ears to the prophets so the calling and the alarm have to be louder and we did experience a loud alarm and a more severe calling. Like Jonathan Cahn's Book (The Harbinger) says that the nation's hedge of protection has been removed from America so therefore the enemies can come in and we are no longer safe.

However, we have been given warnings, each one containing a message.

God did not cause 9/11 to happen, but His hedge of protection has been removed due to our rebellion, our disobedience, our arrogance, our pride, our defiance, our turning away from God's covenant. We drove God out of our nation, we drove Him out of our lives, and even the mention of God or Jesus is becoming more and more prohibited or restricted and even rejected.

9/11 is small compared to a greater judgment to come, if we do not turn.

Nevertheless, if we do not turn to Him, there is going to be something even more severe, something more catastrophic! Believe me, I have seen it in my dreams!

The end times, as described in the Bible, will occur not because it's what God wants for us. It will happen because of mankind's sinfulness. And God will respond as described, in order to save us from ourselves because of His great love for us.

TOUCH NOT MY ANOINTED

They rejected my advice and paid no attention when I corrected them. Therefore, they must eat the bitter fruit of living their own way, choking on their own schemes. Proverbs 1: 30-31-(NIV)

"Hear now my words If there is a prophet among you, I, the Lord, make it known to him in a vision; I speak to him in a dream. "

<u>New International Version</u>
he said, "Listen to my words: "When there is a prophet among you, I, the LORD, reveal myself to them in visions, I speak to them in dreams—Numbers 12:6

As you can see, God has made known to me things to come in my dreams and I am making it known to you, for it is time for me to proclaim His truth and this is what I am doing! The time is now! Nevertheless, I want to tell you what happened in the Bible when a nation repented and turned and God lifted His judgment.

In the Book of Jonah, Jonah was ordered by God to go to the city of Nineveh to prophesy against it for their wickedness. However Jonah instead, sought to flee on a ship from the presence of the Lord by going the opposite direction. In the meantime a huge storm arose and the sailors realized that it was no ordinary storm so they cast lots and they felt that Jonah was to blame. The men on the ship were forced to throw Jonah overboard. Meanwhile God had prepared a big fish to swallow Jonah.

TITANIC/AMERICA

Jonah spent three days and three nights in the belly of a whale. On the third day, Jonah repented and God commanded the fish to spew him out and the fish obeyed. God again ordered Jonah to go to Nineveh to prophesy. This time he obeyed. He went to Nineveh and prophesied. Nineveh fasted and prayed and repented and God lifted the judgment. So you see God is a good God and a God of grace and mercy. He wants us to repent and turn more than we want it for ourselves. So He gives us chances after chances to repent and change. He gives us chances after chances to wake up from our sleep to save us from a greater judgment. God wants us to turn to Him so He can lift the judgment.

- Let's take a look at Israel. God rescued them from slavery. He parted the Red Sea. He provided clothes and food for them. They did not want for anything.

- **Psalms 78:57-(NLT) They turned back and were as faithless as their parents.** They were as undependable as a crooked bow.

- **Psalms 78:58-(NLT)—They angered God by building shrines to other Gods. They made him jealous with their idols.**

- Psalms 78:59-(NLT)—When God heard them, He was very angry and He completely rejected Israel.

Guilt and consequences of it.

- **Numbers 14:43-(KJV)** for the Amalekites and the Canaanites *are* there before you, and ye shall fall by the sword: because ye are turned away from the LORD, therefore the LORD will not be with you.

- **Psalms 125:5-(KJV)** as for such as turn aside unto their crooked ways, the LORD shall lead them forth with the workers of iniquity: *but* peace *shall be* upon Israel.

To make a long story short, God sent prophets after prophets to warn Israel, but they did not take heed so they suffered the consequences of their wicked actions. They were taken by their enemy in captivity and the Lord was not with them because of their disobedience. They were proud and vain and worshipped other gods. They abandoned their God for worthless idols. Read about Jeremiah and other prophets who tried so hard to make them turn, but to no avail.

But even now, God loves His first born Israel, His chosen Nation. Those who curse Israel, He will curse them and those who bless Israel, He will bless them! Israel is still and always be the apple of God's eye!

He said in His word,

Romans 11:1-36 ESV

TITANIC/AMERICA

I ask, then, has God rejected his people? By no means! For I myself am an Israelite, a descendant of Abraham, a member of the tribe of Benjamin. God has not rejected his people whom he foreknew. Do you not know what the Scripture says of Elijah, how he appeals to God against Israel? "Lord, they have killed your prophets, they have demolished your altars, and I alone am left, and they seek my life." But what is God's reply to him? "I have kept for myself seven thousand men who have not bowed the knee to Baal." So too at the present time there is a remnant, chosen by grace. ...

And in time, He alone will make things right with Israel, His chosen nation!

However, getting back to America. If we do not turn from our wicked ways and repent, judgment is headed our way! Someone once said if America does not repent and turn from our wicked ways and God does not proclaim judgment, The Almighty God would have to apologize to "Sodom and Gomorrah!" As you remember in the Bible, Sodom and Gomorrah (Genesis 19) was so wicked that God had the whole town destroyed except for Abraham's nephew, Lot, and his family. We all know the story.

I feel led by my God to pray for America.

2 Chronicles 7:14 New International Version (NIV)

[14] if my people, who are called by my name, will humble

themselves and pray and seek my face and turn from their wicked ways, then I will hear from heaven, and I will forgive their sin and will heal their land.

Father, have mercy on us according to your lovingkindness and tender mercies. Blot out our transgression, wash us of our iniquity and cleanse us of our sin. We have grieved your heart and shamed your name. Look at the bloodshed of our innocent babies. Their blood is crying out. Marriage vows are broken, churches are divided and our lives are polluted! Please Lord, do not give us what we deserve: justice. Extend to us your mercy and grace. Father, you said, (Psalm 33:12a-NKJV), "blessed is the nation whose God is the Lord." We declare and decree that you are the Lord of this nation, we declare and decree that you rule over this land and we declare and decree that we will not bow down to any other god. Father, you also said, Proverbs 14:34-(NKJV), "Righteousness exalts a nation and sin is a reproach to any people." We call in righteousness in this land, we call in love and patience and kindness and humility and holiness and repentant hearts. We call out of the gates of this land, arrogance, pride, greed, anger, divorce, homosexuality, pornography, adultery and abortion and anything that hurts your heart. Wash us with hyssop so we can be clean, cleanse us so we can be whiter than snow. Create in us a clean heart and renew the right spirit. Hide your word in our hearts so we may not sin against you. Lord, forgive us! We turn from our sin with a repentant heart. Father, look at all the people in America that are praying and asking for your forgiveness. In your word, you told Abraham that Sodom and Gomorrah was going to be destroyed and Abraham said if there were even five righteous people, you would not destroy their land. Father, I believe there are many righteous people in this land that love you and are obedient to your word! Do not turn away, Lord, and hear our prayer and answer us.

After I finished praying for America, I was drawn back to the dream that I believed that was given to me by God. As I reflected back, my heart began to pound and I once again became afraid. I fell to my knees once again and I prayed a second prayer for me. In this next chapter, my Lord calmed my fears.

LION OF JUDAH

I told God that I had a dream/vision that I believe was from him and it frightened me and I needed His reassurance that if anything or anyone tried to bother me, and tried to disturb my peace that He would protect me and keep me safe. I also told Him that I know that His Word says that He will protect His people in the event that something catastrophic may happen, but I wanted to be reassured by Him again tonight. Immediately I got up from praying, still caught up in the moment, and I lay back down on the couch and I believe that He put me to sleep. While I was asleep, I also believe that God showed me a vision of me lying on the couch sleeping and a huge male lion was panting by my side. I believe this lion was "the lion of Judah," God Himself, protecting me and keeping me safe. Suddenly, I woke up from my sleep refreshed and renewed and recharged. Suddenly, a message came to me,

"I will be like a lion to you, like a strong lion to you, Ann. I will tear them to pieces, anyone who messes with you. I will carry them off and no one will be able to rescue them from me!" Hosea 5:14 NLT

I was speechless for a moment and I was left without words and my heart was pounding and racing at the same time. I was again caught up in the moment and loving every bit of it! And then, it hit me like it never hit me before that my God, my Father, who is the creator of this universe answered my prayers immediately. He let me know that He loved me and that He would always protect me in time of trouble along with His people!

Wow! What an awesome God! I knew that He loved me before, but this time it was different somehow—in a way that I cannot explain!! I wanted to laugh, I wanted to shout out loud, but if I did, I knew that people would hear me. But somehow at this moment, I did not care if anyone heard me, and I wanted to rejoice and I did! I could no longer hold it in. I stood up from my chair which was in front of my laptop computer and I just had a party all by myself!! I danced and praised the Lord and I shouted and I did not care who heard me! I realized at that very moment that I was blessed beyond measure, that I was greatly blessed, highly favored and deeply loved by "the God of this universe!" I was intrigued and amused and excited to the point that I almost could not stop praising Him! I wanted this feeling to last forever! I sensed that an open heaven was abiding in my home. It was like an Oasis of Heaven. I felt renewed and re-fired and refreshed and charged in the spirit! How awesome is that!!

I will always remember that whatever tries to harm me, (or you beloved, as a child of God), we have the Living God on our side, whether it would be a dream or if it is real! God did not give me a spirit of fear, but of power and love and a sound mind. How awesome is that, that God (Himself) let me know that whatever difficulty, hardship, or pain, comes my (our) way whether it has anything to

◄ TOUCH NOT MY ANOINTED

do with me or our nation that he will be my refuge and my high tower and no weapon formed against me shall prosper and all tongues that rise up against me, I will condemn. In other words, God is not only saying this to me but I believe that he is saying that to all his people. The bottom line is if you have asked God into your life, He will protect you in time of trouble. I believe God is speaking through me to all His people!

I also had one other dream and I believe I can share this one also. Again, God is warning me of things to come if we do not turn! Here is the dream!

Hundreds of people were in a huge building. It was in the winter time because we were cold and there was no heat or electricity. I sensed it was like a nuclear war going on outside and we were locked inside this building. It was sooo dark in this building, I could not see any faces. We had no food and no light, and the only clothes we had was what we were wearing. The windows seemed to be all boarded up and we were not able to see on the outside. The doors were locked and no one could come in or go out. Meanwhile, in the corner of the room, I saw a man who came from nowhere, he just appeared out of nowhere and of all the hundreds of people that were locked in this huge room, he singled me out and walked up to me and asked me if I would like to share his covering. He stared into my eyes, as if he was waiting for my response. Although it was dark in this room, His face radiated with light and it lit up the entire room.

I was speechless and baffled, and then it hit me all at once like a tidal wave. That man who asked me if I wanted to share his blanket, I believe, was Jesus!! As he paused for a moment staring into my eyes, I could not speak. My heart was pounding and my palms were sweating, and suddenly I agreed to share his blanket and He lay down beside me. Then I woke up from this dream.

Once again, I repeat. I believed this man was Jesus. He let me know that whatever is happening, whether it is inside or outside, whether it was a nuclear war or hardship or pain, He would protect me!! He let me know that I had nothing to fear and I would not be alone in this struggle! He would be with me!

I believe that dream was a message of great importance! I also believe that this was a message of judgment—once again another dream that holds the key to America's future. I hesitate to say this, but I believe that God was preparing me for what is about to come.

In any case, I have prayed and repented for our nation and I asked God to extend to us not judgment but grace and mercy!! May God help us!! If you think this dream was bad, it was nothing compared to the first one "Titanic"! (However, read 2 Chronicles 7: 14)

Beloved, if you have not asked Jesus into your life, do it right now, and I believe that whatever disaster comes upon this nation, you will be protected!! In Revelation 3:10—11a—it says

"Because you have obeyed my command to persevere, I will protect you from the great time of testing that will come upon the whole world to test those who belong to this world. I am coming soon! Hold on to what you have so that no one will take away your crown!!"

Roman 10:9-10 (NIV) says:

If you declare with your mouth that Jesus is Lord and believe in your heart that Jesus was raised from the dead, you will be saved!! If you have prayed that Prayer, you are saved and all the angels in heaven are having a party because your name is now written in the Lamb's book of life!! When testing comes for this world, beloved, God will protect you!!

"Sometimes I feel like I do not have anyone else, only God, but having Him is more than having everything."

Even when I was small, I used to scare my mom with all the dreams I would have and she could not handle it. It was so hard for her to hear the things God was speaking to me even before I knew Him.

I REMEMBER TELLING MY MOM WHEN I WAS AT HOME IN TENNESSEE THAT I SENSED IN MY HEART, THERE IS A WILL FOR MY LIFE GREATER THAN MY FEAR OF WHAT PEOPLE MAY THINK OR DO.

My mom just looked at me as if to say, "I am going to pray

long and hard for you every day because, daughter, you are a piece of work."

Mom used to be afraid for me because I was different than my siblings and no matter how hard she tried, she could not understand me, but then again, maybe she did understand me because I was in some way just like her. Just maybe?

I know that I may sometime sound prideful but prideful I am not. However, I am so confident of my Father's love that I will not walk in fear because God is for me and not against me. Maybe my mom was afraid for me when I was young but I was never afraid then and I choose not to be afraid now. Walking in faith and not fear is my choice. I choose not to ever be afraid!

If God does allow difficulty, hardship and pain to come into my life, it is for a good reason. He is trying to develop my character and strengthen my faith. Although the difficulty and hardship and pain is not my identity; however, it does identify with whom I am becoming. Like Graham Cooke said, "It is the process that makes you rich, in that if God had not allowed you to go through it, your faith would not be strengthened and your character would not have been developed. This in turn, causes you to become more like Jesus. The bottom line is (I repeat) like Graham Cooke said,

"It is the process that makes you rich."

TOUCH NOT MY ANOINTED

Why would I fear anything, because my God is in control even when it seems like He is not. Although sometimes fear tries to creep upon me, I just give that fear to God and command it to leave.

I am at a point in my life that when people treat me unfairly, I pray that God will extend to them grace and mercy and not judgment. I have seen the results of God's justice to all who have mistreated me and His children. However, I can only speak for myself.

ORDINARY PEOPLE

Sometimes I have no idea what God is trying to say to me in my dreams but sometimes He makes it very clear to me. I pray all the time that I would get better at interpreting all of them. I pray that God would give me the spirit of Daniel. (Read the Book of Daniel in the Bible). God gave him the gift of interpreting dreams. It seems like in these end times, I am gaining ground in the interpretation of many of my dreams. ☺

God speaks to the prophets. He sometimes talks to me as He talked to them. As He spoke to Moses and Jeremiah and Daniel and Joseph and also Mary (mother of Jesus) in the Bible, and as you see, He also speaks to me.

In Exodus chapter 3 it tells about Moses being in the desert and he came upon a burning bush and the angel of the Lord appeared to Moses in the flame of fire out of the midst of the bush and the fire was burning but it was not consumed and God called him and Moses said, "Here I am." To make a long story short, God asked Moses to go back to Egypt and talk to pharaoh about freeing His people. Moses had big doubts about his ability to lead. He resisted God, bringing up his unworthiness and lack of authority and his fear of the people, but in the end, God used him and his brother, Aaron, to free His people. It was not easy; it was a major undertaking. Every time Moses went to talk to

◄ TOUCH NOT MY ANOINTED

Pharaoh about freeing God's people, Pharaoh's heart was hardened. Eventually after ten plagues, God's people were freed.

The remainder of Exodus should give people with similar doubts great hope. Read the Book of Exodus and you will enjoy how God used someone who could not even see himself as a deliverer of God's people. However, God came through big time for Moses. Why? Moses was God's anointed. If you read 1 Corinthians 1: 26-29-(NLT), God chose things the world considers foolish to shame those who think that they are wise, and He chose the things that are powerless to shame those who are powerful. God chose things that are despised by the world, things counted as nothing at all, and used them to bring to nothing all that the world considers important. As a result, no one can ever boast in the presence of God.

When you check out the Bible, you will see on many occasions that God used those people that most people would not give a second thought, and those were the people He used to do something powerful. Let me give you an example. In 2 Kings 5:15 the Bible tells that Naaman was a great man in Syria when he got leprosy. A servant girl whom he had captured from Israel told Naaman's wife that the prophet Elisha could heal him from leprosy. Because Naaman was willing to listen to a servant girl, not only was he healed and his life was spared but he came to know the one true God. What a miracle!!!

I believe that God often speaks through those to whom few are willing to listen. I have come to a conclusion, to hear God, you have to listen to the meek and humble. I have learned through my experience that you never dismiss people because they are not educated and they do not have a title by their name. Every person that you encounter should be considered sacred.

In the Bible and in real life, God uses ordinary people to carry out His supernatural extraordinary plan.

Look at me. I am just as ordinary as ordinary could be and God is using me. If he is using me, He can use anyone, whether you are black or white, old or young—as long as you have a pulse, God can use you (See 1Corinthians 1:27).

May I repeat, He is using those things the world sees as foolish to shame those who are powerful. God uses things counted as nothing at all to bring to nothing what the world considers important.

I am like the servant girl whom God used to give Naaman this message of hope and by doing this, Naaman was healed and he came to know the one true living God. How awesome is that!!

I believe that God speaks to me through my dreams. Someone once told me that He speaks to you through your dreams if you can't hear His voice. I do not know how true that is. Even before I was born again (as you have learned earlier) God would speak to me. He speaks to me about my family, my friends and even people that I do not know. Also at times, I believe that God gives me words to speak to people and sometimes when that happens, the people that I speak to tend to dismiss me because I do not have a title beside my name or maybe just maybe because of my color. However, like Charles Stanley said, "Do what God tells you to do and leave the consequences to Him." I have decided to do just that!

"I have come to my own conclusion-When God gives me a word for someone and they do not receive it, they are rejecting God not me!"

DREAMS AND VISIONS

You see God spoke to Moses in a burning bush and He speaks to me in prophetic words and dreams and visions. You may not see the similarity but I do.

You see, not only does God gives me prophetic words for people, but I will ask God for something and He usually puts me to sleep and then He will answer me in my dream.

I would like to give you an example of God speaking to me in another one of my dreams. I am not going to go into details, but one time I had voted for this one president and I prayed and prayed and prayed God's Word and yet, the person I voted for president did not win. I fell to my knees and asked God 'where did I go wrong?' I told Him that when I pray His word and have faith to believe it, I will have it; but this time I did not get what I prayed for. When I pray for something, I expect that I will get what I ask for because I believe. I am like Abraham, his body was as good as dead when God told him that he would be the father of nations. Abraham did not stagger at the promise, but he believed God and Abraham became the father of nations. I am like Abraham, when I pray I believe that God answers my prayers. I believe God, and I do not stagger at His promises (Read Romans 4:20 about Abraham). When I pray, I expect everything I pray to come to pass because I know that God cannot lie; what God says, He will do. I believe that with all of my heart. I am not moved by my feelings, nor moved by what people say, but I am only moved by God's word and what His word says, "Pray and believe that you will receive it and you shall have what you ask" (Mark 11:24 NKJ).

I guess I did not understand why I prayed God's Word and He did not seem to perform it this time.

I cried all night and I continued to pour out my heart to God asking Him where I went wrong and what I needed to do to bring about a different outcome? When I prayed I even repented for hidden sins that I did not know about. I did everything I knew to do and still my prayers were not answered. My heart was troubled like a wild sea in a raging storm and I continued to weep without signs of letting up.

Once again, I believe that God put me to sleep and He gave me a dream.

I believe that He finally put me to sleep and He gave me a dream. In this dream I was standing in front of my house and a surveyor came up to me and said, 'That land is corrupt and wicked.' He was pointing to another location and I stated that was not my land, I told him that where I am standing is my land and He said in the dream, "Yes, I know, your land is good and pure and positive but that land (as he pointed) is wicked." I immediately awoke from the dream and I asked God to explain to me what he was trying to say in this dream and it was so clear. I believed that God said,

DREAMS AND VISIONS

"I gave them what they wanted."

Like in the Bible, the Israelites asked for a king even though God was their king; but He gave them what they asked for even though He did not approve. (Read 1 Samuel in the Bible) I said that to say this: I do not believe this president was His choice. I believe that He gave the people what they wanted like He did with the Israelites. I do believe that particular president was not his choice; it was the people's choice. Wow, that was an eye opener. I remember a lot of people used to say that whoever becomes president is the one that God chooses because God is always in control. Yes, maybe God chose him, but it was not his choice, nor his perfect will. It was the people's choice. In other words, He gave the people what they wanted. In any event, after God had given me that dream, my heart was comforted and joy once again flooded my soul with singing and my mourning turned into dancing. He heard me from His sanctuary and my cry to Him reached his ears and He answered me, not because he had to, but because He wanted to. Thank you, my precious Lord, my Savior and my best friend. Who is like the Lord?

I learned something from that situation and that is: God sometimes gives us what we ask for, even though it is not His choice. Most of the time when God gives us what we want, but not His choice, we usually regret it.

Nevertheless, no matter who becomes president, we are called to pray for our leaders (1 Timothy 2:1-4). We are to

pray for them to be a catalyst to bring about change for our nation. That is in God's Word and we have to obey it. We have to honor God's Word.

If I may, I would like to share with you a vision that I had in 2012. I have shared with you many of my dreams and now let me also share with you one of the visions that God put on my heart.

I remember seeing a young lady in the hallway at the church I was attending and all of a sudden I saw in the spirit a baby in her stomach. Her belly was big and she appeared pregnant. I had seen her the day before and her belly was flat and I looked away and when I looked back, her belly was flat again. At first I thought my eyes were playing tricks on me. I did not understand what just happened for several months. In church, I usually sit in the same place with my friend Debra, but for some reason, on this particular day, I sat in a different place and guess who came and sat by me? It was the same lady I had seen in the hallway pregnant in the spirit. She and her husband came and sat beside me. I believe that God asked me to tell her at this time what I had seen in the spirit months ago and when the service was over, I wrote her a note telling her that I saw her pregnant in the spirit. I gave her this note and she passed it to her husband and then she whispered to me telling me she just found out that she was pregnant the day before. She was amazed! Her name is Nichole. Now she has a beautiful baby girl.

I used to wonder why God was always on my case before I got saved and now I think I know. He had deposited gifts and talents and potential and seeds of greatness inside of me even before I was formed in my mom's womb, and He was trying to protect His investment. Say for instance, suppose you would buy a house. Would you just let the house go without taking care of it?

Of course not, you would take care of your house. You would buy insurance for the house and do everything you need to do to protect this huge investment. You see, to God we are much more valuable than a house; we are a spirit who has a soul who lives in this body and God wants to protect His investments. However, even before I asked Him into my life, it was as if God was protecting His investment not only because of the gift but it was because He loves me. He loves all of His creation!

I know what I know and I know this is true!!!

You see, God is so good and He loves me and He also wants to protect His investments.

I would like to take a couple of minutes to say to my God how much I love Him. Since I have asked God into my life, my life is so fulfilling and rewarding and I have so much peace and contentment. His love feels like a river flowing from His heart to mine, and His love and His words bubble out of me to give people hope.

◂ TOUCH NOT MY ANOINTED

Oh God, I just want you. I always want to be in your presence. Who am I that you love me so much? What would I do, Lord, if I did not have you? I would not want to live. I cannot imagine my life without you. Your love is healing and trusting and unfailing. My heart beats for you and you alone. If I ever thought that I was in love before, I was deceived. God, you are the kindest person I have ever met. You are and have been relentlessly kind to me, day after day, week after week and year after year. You are generous. You are eternal, everlasting, and you are always the same. You never gave up on me, even when I gave up on myself. I know that I have broken your heart a thousand times over but you never let me go. Hold on to me, God, and do not let me lose my way, for your way is perfect. Father, in your word you asked Ezekiel to breathe on the dry bones and bring them back to life. I ask you, Father, to breathe on me and all of your creation at this very moment and cultivate in each one of us a thirst and a hunger and a craving and an intimacy with you beyond our wildest imagination. I pray that I will never hold back and I will always give you everything, and everything is a lesser thing compared to you. Lord, you are everything I need. You are everything that anyone needs.

Last but not least, your love for us (your creation and especially your children) is rigid, inflexible, immovable and real! Thank You!

One day when I was reading God's word it read, (God was talking about Israel)

DREAMS AND VISIONS

"I will bless those who bless you and I will curse those who curse you."

In my spirit, I heard God say, "Ann, I feel the same way about you as I do about my first born (Israel). If anyone blesses you, I will bless them and if any one curses you, I will definitely curse them. Ann, I always hear your prayer and I will always answer it and I will always watch over you because you are dear to my heart. You are my treasure."

As I heard these words from the heart of God, I knew that I was so special to Him and I do not even know why except when God looks at me, He sees His son Jesus and also I have realized that being kind is who He is!! He is to me the kindest person I have ever known, He is the wisest person I have ever known. His wisdom I cannot even fathom. As my eyes were filling up with tears, knowing how much He loves me, there was no word that would even scratch the surface of what I was feeling for Him. To the faithful, He shows Himself faithful, to those with integrity, He shows integrity and to the pure, He shows Himself to be pure; but to the wicked, He shows Himself hostile. I know that I am not perfect but I believe I have a pure perfect heart toward Him.

In the Bible, Joseph, among others, was not perfect but I believe that he had a perfect heart toward God.

Sometimes I compare myself to Joseph in the Bible. Joseph's

father's name was Jacob. Jacob had many sons but his favorite son was Joseph, because he had him in his old age. I also believe that I was my father's favorite (my earthly father) when I was small.

Joseph had prophetic dreams. God revealed Joseph's future by way of two dreams. Young Joseph was naïve and he told his dreams to his brothers and these dreams made them hate him all the more. Eventually the brothers sold him into slavery and they told their father that Joseph was killed. However, Joseph ended up in prison in Egypt because of lies; but later he became a careful, prudent leader who would emerge from prison years later to lead Egypt. He was the second highest ranking person in Egypt. Read all about Joseph in Genesis, starting in Chapter 37. You will really enjoy it.

My life was not totally similar to Joseph, but there were some similarities. Basically, we dreamed a lot, both of us did. I believed our dreams were prophetic and God spoke to us about our future in our dreams. However, Joseph could interpret his dreams and I cannot, at least not all of them yet.

Joseph's brothers did not care for him because they thought that their father gave him special attention; and in reality, their father did. I may be wrong, but I never thought that I was liked by most of my family. When I was small and even in my later years I did not feel love from some of my family members. Although I know that they did love me, I do not know if they actually liked me. Then again, maybe I was not the easiest person to love or like.

I was very close to my dad and my brother, Rex. I believe that, like Joseph, I was my dad's favorite. I could tell him anything and he would listen. I do not know how much he understood but I do know that he was a good listener. I guess I was close to my dad because I was a sick child and maybe all the attention I received from him could possibly have caused my siblings to feel jealous. When I was small, I did not make the connection. However, hindsight is 20/20.

As I write my book, I realize that I have more in common with Joseph than I thought.

As I mentioned earlier (and I do not want to bore you with this by repeating myself), if you have children and they dream a lot, do not just dismiss it, because their dreams just may be from God. At first, my mom would listen to my dreams and she would allow me to share them but as time passed she thought that they were more or less nightmares that I should not share with anyone but her. However over a process of time, she did not even want to hear them so I dreamed and pondered them in my heart and I began to notice that most of them would come to pass. I am saying that to say this and it bears repeating.

When you have a young child who dreams quite a bit, do not always dismiss it as nothing. On the contrary, the dreams could be a message or a warning from God.

I read a book by Herman Riffel and he said that we dream for an hour or more per night, and about three years out of our entire life is spent dreaming. Doesn't that speak loud and clear, and doesn't that say surely there is a purpose in our dreams? "In the last days God says, 'I will pour out my spirit on all people. Your sons and your daughters will prophesy, your young men will see visions and your old men will dream dreams'" Acts 2:17-(NLT). There is no hint that God intended to stop using these dreams to speak to His people.

Some of your children's dreams could be a warning or a sign, or it could be God's message to this child's future, or it also could be a result of what they ate before they went to bed. Pray for sharp discernment.

As I mentioned earlier, I was quite different from my siblings for it seemed my whole life was about dreams and visions. I do not know whether or not my siblings dreamed; but if they did, they did not take note of it like I did. Not only was my personality different from my sisters, I looked different from all my sisters except for Freda. She and I looked a lot alike but were totally different in character and personality. Freda was outgoing and the life of a party and she was a natural born leader. Freda was beautiful! And she still is. Especially when she became a teenager. She had long hair and a beautiful figure and she had this gifted personality to go with it. I was always so proud that she was my sister.

DREAMS AND VISIONS

On the other hand, I was shy and insecure. I was not outgoing, nor gregarious and was extremely introverted! I was also very uncomfortable when I was around a crowd. To be exact, I was the ultimate wallflower. I did not have much to say but I did a lot of thinking. The one thing (among many) that set me apart from all of my sisters was my many dreams. Sometimes in these dreams, it seemed that God was speaking directly to me, as you know. In my family, I would probably say that I was considered a misfit!

A MISFIT TO MEN, BUT BY GOD'S STANDARD, A GIANT IN THE EYES OF HEAVEN.

THAT IS MY GOAL, TO BE A GIANT IN THE EYES OF HEAVEN. JOSEPH WAS!!! JESUS WAS!!! I WANT TO BE!

In my family, I always felt as though I was watching from the outside and I had no inside connection except for maybe my dad.

Freda would sometimes tell me that I appeared to live in a world of my own. She did not seem to like that at all. It almost seemed like it really bothered her, especially when she became a teenager. I used to sense that she did not care for me at all.

However, in my latter years, I am closer to Freda than I am anyone else in my family. She is now a huge blessing in my life! I thank God every day for her.

As I spoke earlier, in my family you would say that I was in a way a "misfit." I really did not fit in.

I looked up misfit in the dictionary and I am surprised that my picture was not there. It said that misfit was something that fits badly, a person who is poorly adjusted to a

situation or to an environment. You see, I was not only a misfit in my family but it seems like I have been a misfit all my life. However I have come to realize that I am in the wrong environment! I was in the wrong family. It also seemed that I was born at the wrong time.

I was supposed to be born way back when. But as you read on, I believe that you will understand what seems to have happened.

I just did not seem to fit in. Even today I seem to think differently from my peers and even my friends and my family. I also seem to think differently from some of my Christian friends. Even though it took me forever to finally meet someone who understands me, I am so blessed that He is in my life now, and He always will be.

I realized now that uniqueness makes you rich.

Have you guessed who this person is? His name is Jesus. He loves me the way I am. He made me this way and He loves me in spite of me. I have said that to say this, that even though I am different than most, my Father is using me and He is molding me to come up higher to be like His Son, Jesus. You may think that you are a misfit, but to God you are perfect. He will be your potter and you will be the clay and He can mold you to be the person He has called you to be. I realized that if you are a misfit, you are not called to be part of a group, you are called to lead the group. You were a misfit because you were chosen by God to be different, but different in a good way. As I mentioned before, look at Jesus; He was different, but a good different.

Uniqueness makes you rich

Because He (Jesus) was brilliant. He was and is now the wisest man who ever lived and I believe that He was, by some, called a misfit because they could not squeeze Him in their mold and He would not bow down to their pressure to be like them. He was molded by God, and not by man.

When God asks you to do some things for Him, they will not be reasonable but will seem totally impossible. You will feel like you cannot do it-

BUT GOD CAN—You will say to God "I cannot do it" and He will say, "YOU ARE PERFECT FOR ME." You are a perfect fit!

When God asked me to write this book, I was in shock because a writer is a reader and a reader, I am not! I asked God, "How could I do this?" and He said, "You will not do it, I will!!"

Even today, I cannot compute it in my head why my God chased me down for so many years and never would let me go. The only answer that I could come up with was He had a plan for me to write. I also believe my mom must have prayed for me more than for my siblings. As I mentioned earlier, she would always tell me that I trusted people too much and that I always took people at face value. She would sometimes tell me that she hoped that I would grow out of this child-like stage so people would not take advantage of me when I got older.

She (Mom) insisted that I would be like a lamb among wolves in the world but I knew deep inside of me that I would have a lion panting by my side. Do not ask me how I knew that, I just did. I would always ponder that in my heart and I now know the lion would be God!!

My mom used to say that I was always so pure in my thinking and so transparent in my heart that it sometimes scared her.

I may be wrong, but I believe that God sees that quality of purity in me and I believe that He is and was deeply moved by it, even now!

WHEN I WAS SIXTEEN YEARS OLD, I WOULD FOLLOW MOM AROUND AND FIND WHERE SHE WOULD GO TO BE ALONE WITH HER GOD.

I would watch my mom worship God and would be drawn into her passion for Him. Once she discovered that I was watching her, she became agitated and would run me away. I was the only child who would prefer being with my mom over doing anything else. Like I said before, I was different than the rest of the children. They would prefer watching television or playing outside. On the other hand, I would prefer being around her. However, I was always a puzzle to her. She could not understand me. At least that is the way it seemed. Sometimes I would see her looking at me in a way that if that look could speak, I believe that it would say, "My child, my beautiful daughter, I wish I could understand you, but I love you anyway, because you are mine" (on the other hand, she could have been thinking something totally different). She would then walk up to me and take my hand in her hand and comfort me with her smile. I always loved her smile, because when she smiled, it lit up the whole room. Her smile could launch a thousand ships. My mom was tall and slim and beautiful.

Everywhere we went she would get attention from men and women. She reminded me of First Lady, Jacqueline Kennedy, President John F. Kennedy's wife. I admired them both!

My mom was not much into hugging, but her smile was sometimes better than a hug. You see, moms' mom, which would have been my grandmother, died in childbirth and the baby she was carrying died also. My mom was about five years old when her mom died so my mom was raised without a mother. She was the youngest, so one of her oldest sisters took her in and raised her. My mom had many sisters but I remember mom telling me that she looked different than the rest of her sisters. She was much darker in color and she sometimes felt like she was the black sheep of her family. I believe because of her growing up without her natural mother and being different not only in color but in character, this led her to God. Although she did not go to church, she had a strong, deep and intimate relationship with Him. As I am writing my book, I am beginning to understand my mom more today than I have before. I see a resemblance between her and me. She was different than the rest of her sisters just as I was different from my sisters. In any event, sometimes I caught my mom staring at me and I believe now I know why. She was seeing herself in me when she was growing up. I never realized that before, until now, this very moment. I believe that Mom wanted to tell me that her childhood was a twin image of mine; but she always remained silent. In any case, she could never get up the nerve, although I wished she had.

As I continue to write, I believe God is opening my eyes, causing thoughts to flood my heart with revelation.

I am actually realizing at this moment, that my mom and I were very much alike in many ways. I wonder did she have prophetic dreams but did not tell us? Wow, that is a huge mystery!! These thoughts will be forever planted in the incubation of my mind quietly, secretly and silently (I guess not secretly).

In any event, I guess I am saying that to say this, I believe my mom prayed for me more than the other children because she could see secretly that I was like her in many ways. She could see that I was different and she knew that my character required her to pray that the will of God would come forth in my life.

I believe that Mom quietly knew that my life was marked by God and He had chosen me to be set apart for His glory. I may be wrong, but I really believe that this is the reason God pursued me with a passion because of her prayers. I am not saying that He did not pursue my siblings because honestly, I do not know. However, I cannot speak for them, I can only speak for myself.

BUT THE HARD TRUTH IS, IT TOOK YEARS BEFORE I RECEIVED JESUS IN MY LIFE. ALTHOUGH I SAW JESUS' HAND UPON MY LIFE, I WAS STILL NOT IMPRESSED. I WAS FOOLISH AND STUPID. I WAS CLEVER ENOUGH TO DO WRONG, BUT I HAD NO IDEA HOW TO DO RIGHT. I WAS BLIND TO THE TRUTH. MY REBELLION WAS GREAT AND MY SINS WERE MANY AND I REFUSED TO BE CORRECTED AND REFUSED TO TURN FROM MY SIN. MY FACE WAS LIKE A STONE AND I WAS DETERMINED TO DO WRONG.

You know beloved, through all this I realize that

"IF I ASCEND INTO HEAVEN, GOD WOULD BE WITH ME, IF I MAKE MY BED IN HELL, BEHOLD, HE IS THERE, IF I TAKE THE WINGS OF THE MORNING, AND DWELL IN THE UTTERMOST PARTS OF THE SEA, EVEN THERE, HIS HAND SHALL LEAD ME AND HIS RIGHT HAND SHALL HOLD ME AND THE DARKNESS SHALL NOT FALL

ON ME AND EVEN THE NIGHT SHALL BE LIGHT ABOUT ME AND THE DARKNESS SHALL NOT HIDE FROM YOU, FOR YOU FORMED MY INWARD PARTS, AND YOU COVERED ME IN MY MOM'S WOMB. I AM FEARFULLY AND WONDERFULLY MADE" Psalm 139:8 (paraphrased).

I do not understand a lot of things but I do understand one thing and that is—"I have a gift (an ancient gift) and God has gone out of His way to protect this gift." I believe that it is very valuable to Him and He will not rest until this gift that is in me is proclaimed and recognized. I am not one hundred percent sure what this gift is or what it is going to be but I have a good idea now of what He has called me to do. I have seen the proof and I have showed you just a fraction of what He has shown me. Beloved, I would like to make it clear to you. I may have given you the impression that God protects my gift but to be honest with you, I know that He loves me far more than my gift. He protects me because He really loves me. However, the gift is important also. I just wanted to clear that up.

I remember reading an article by Kim Clement and when I read this article, my spirit leaped! I believe that it was bearing witness to the truth, God's truth. It was as though my God was speaking directly to me and I realized that (knowing this truth) was going to be a catalyst for my spiritual development.

Let me tell you what his article said. Kim Clement was speaking to God's children.

"You are a unique copy of an ancient gift, whether it's the ancient gift of Joseph, Jeremiah, or the ancient gift of Isaiah, or even Mary (Mother of Jesus) or Daniel." Kim went on to say that he believes that when Daniel died, his gift never died. He believes that we are a unique copy of one of those gifts. "Therefore, you are going to behave as your brothers and forefathers behaved." Kim went on to say that there are so many churches trying to be prophetic without the ingredients (the gifts of faith). It takes a special faith to be prophetic; it takes a special vision to be prophetic. What is prophetic? It means that you see further and look from above at the whole picture, instead of from a limited (religious) viewpoint. According to Kim Clement, there are three kinds of sight: eyesight, insight, and foresight.

"Insight is the sight inside your head, and foresight is to see ahead in time, and catch a glimpse of yourself in the future with a lot more faith than you have now. If you catch a glimpse of what you look like in the future, it is the most powerful and most wonderful thing, and it will revolutionize your life. You will begin to praise Him for the things yet to come."

As I write, I am beginning to realize more and more why I seem so different, why I seemed to be a misfit. I am different because of an ancient gift that was passed on to me when they died (our forefathers—Jeremiah and Daniel or even Joseph).

I believe that my gift is not traditional but it is ancient, from years ago, and I believe my mom had this same gift.

A MISFIT TO MEN, BUT BY GOD'S STANDARD, A GIANT IN THE EYES OF HEAVEN.

It is almost like new pages of my life are beginning to open up and I am beginning to see clearer now why I am not so easily accepted and why I have never seemed to fit in. In fact, I realize that I don't think normally; I seem to think supernaturally.

When I read this article, I could not get it out of my mind. My heart was pounding and I was amused and intrigued at the same time. It was as if God was speaking directly to me. I paused for a moment, considering everything that Kim Clement had spoken. I was so caught up in the moment and I believed that the mystery had been resolved and the message was revealed.

I believe that God was speaking to me loud and clear. Again, I may sound prideful but prideful, I am not. I am confident of my God and what He is saying to me. I truly believe that I do have Joseph's gift or Jeremiah's or even a little of both. I also believe that I have a gift of vision and the gift of faith. Kim said to be prophetic, you will need them both. When God tells me something, I see the invisible so therefore I will have the impossible.

When I read that article, it reminded me again of Mary (the mother of Jesus) when the angel told her that she was going to have a baby and the baby's name would be Jesus and He also told Mary that her cousin Elizabeth was pregnant in her old age.(If you have not read the book of Luke, please read it.) I am not trying to compare myself to Mary; I am just trying to make a point. Mary had a gift of faith and also she had vision. She believed what the angel told her and she saw the vision and she ran with it. I believe according to the world's standard that she would be called a misfit. Why? Because when the angel told her that she would be the mother of Messiah, she believed!! I know I tend to go on and on about Mary, the mother of Jesus, but I sincerely know that she was definitely conceived for the purpose of the will of God and so was I! Beloved, believe me when I say, "So are you! "When Mary decided to travel to visit Elizabeth, when Mary spoke to Elizabeth, the baby leaped in Elizabeth's womb. They both were pregnant with a purpose and they both had faith and vision to believe what the angel had prophesied over them. I believe that when you are pregnant (spiritually) with a purpose, you need to be around people who are also pregnant with a purpose to make your *'baby leap'.* Sometimes you can be around someone and the purpose inside seems stagnant or even dead. Those people are not pregnant with God's purpose and they do not understand who you are and where you are going. Since they do not understand it, some people will reject it and I can now understand why. Because they are not pregnant with faith and vision, they do not see what you see and they do not believe what you believe so they literally reject what you are telling them because they can't see it. Their spiritual eyes are not open to it, at least not yet. However to the world and even to some Christians, they will see you as a misfit—the one who does not fit in because you are pregnant with a purpose and they are not. Earlier when I mentioned about going to the Prophetic Conference, those prophets were pregnant and they made my baby leap! It was sooo meaningful to me to finally hear a confirmation of what I believed God had already spoken to my heart! How awesome is that! I want to do great things for God and not lose the challenge of doing even greater things! I believe in a bigger story and that bigger story is coming and I know that it is even bigger than this book!

I guess I said all that to say this, God is and has always protected me and now I am beginning to understand why. As I write, God is giving me revelation of just what my gift is and I do believe that it is a gift of faith and also a gift of vision which goes along with prophecy.

God is protecting His gift, His anointing, and nothing, absolutely nothing is going to stop His gift from operating!!!

I believe if anyone tries to get in the way of my gift that I have received from God, He will go out of His way to shield me and protect me and that is what he did in my life when my boyfriend, Harvey, wanted me to get high on drugs. If I had decided to do those drugs, I could have died.

I believe that my God protected me then and He protects me now. I believe it was the gift that He is protecting (the Ancient Gift) because it is so valuable to my God but most of all He is protecting the disciple whom Jesus loves (me). I believe that God hates anyone who tries to get in the way of the purpose and the plan that He has for His children, including myself.

TOUCH NOT MY ANOINTED

I believe that nothing makes God angrier than someone trying to stop the call that God has on your life or interferes with your relationship to Him!! I believe that He hates that.

I know one thing and that is, what God has for you will come to pass. No one, absolutely no one can stop it, although it may blocked, hindered or held back for a season, or you may even be called a misfit.

But this I know, the plan that God has for will come to pass with a vengeance!

"Touch not my anointed!"

My beloved, hear my heart. If you have not asked Jesus into your heart, let's take a minute and do it right now. Just repeat after me.

"Jesus come into my heart and be my Lord and be my Savior. Forgive me for my sins. I know that you died on the cross but in three days, you were raised from the dead.

Right now you are sitting at the right hand of our father interceding on my behalf, In Jesus' name I pray, Amen!!"

If you have prayed that and you were sincere in your heart, you are saved!! All of Heaven is having a party on your behalf and like my former pastor would say, all of your sins have been erased. If you would die today, you know exactly where you would go. Your spirit would go straight to Heaven!!! Absent from the body is in the presence of the Lord.

How awesome is that!

SUBMIT TO GOD AND YOU WILL HAVE PEACE

Listen, beloved, listen to me. Submit to God and you will have peace. Listen to His instructions, and store them in your heart, and always have them ready on your lips. I am teaching you today so you will always trust in the Lord.

If you stray from the right path, return quickly to the Almighty. You will be restored—so clean up your life. If you give up your lust for money and throw your precious gold into the river, the Almighty God Himself will be your treasure. He will be your precious silver! And you will then take delight in the Almighty and look up to God. You will pray to Him and He will hear you, and you will fulfill your vows to Him. You will succeed in whatever you choose to do, and light will shine on the road ahead of you. If people are in trouble and you ask Him to help them, the Almighty will save them. Even sinners will be rescued because your hands are pure (Job 22: 25-30).

ANN'S PRAYER TO THE ALMIGHTY

You take no delight in sacrifices or offerings. Now that you made me listen, I finally understand. You do not require burnt offerings or sin offerings. I take joy in doing your will and, my God, your instructions are written on my heart. I have told all your people about your justice and I have not been afraid to speak out as you, O Lord, well know. I have not kept the good news of your justice hidden in my heart and I have talked about your faithfulness and saving power. I also have told everyone in the great assembly of your unfailing love and faithfulness. Lord, since I have known you, I have and will always try my best to let your wisdom guide my thoughts and actions though sometimes I have noticed that it did not work. But when I sought you concerning this issue, you did not judge me, but you looked beyond my imperfection and flaws and blemishes and reminded me that I was not perfect and you loved me and you did not judge me!

Lord, thank you for your mercy and grace. I will forever be thankful.

Lord, I believe that you have given me a compelling message to give your people concerning America. My responsibility is to be obedient to you and leave the consequences also to you! I believe these dreams that you have given me hold a key to our (America's) future. They are not only mystery but a message, an alarm or a warning! I hope that your people realize that it is not really about (me) the messenger, it is about the message!

"LORD, MY PRECIOUS ALMIGHTY, I LOVE YOU WITH ALL OF MY HEART AND SOUL AND MIND. LORD, I LOVE YOU MORE THAN LIFE ITSELF. YOU HAVE GIVEN ME, YOUR SERVANT, IF I AM NOT MISTAKEN, GREAT RESPONSIBILITIES TO RELAY YOUR MESSAGE AND YET I SEEM LIKE A CHILD IN THE SPIRIT AND I AM NOT 100% SURE HOW TO CARRY IT OUT. TEACH ME, LORD, HOW TO HEAR YOUR VOICE AND FOLLOW YOU AND TRUST IN YOU ALL THE DAYS OF MY LIFE, NEVER HOLDING BACK AND GIVING YOU EVERYTHING. AFTER ALL, FATHER, FROM THE VERY BEGINNING, ALL YOU EVER WANTED FROM ME WAS MY HEART! O LORD MY GOD, YOU HAVE PERFORMED MANY WONDERS FOR ME. YOUR PLANS FOR ME ARE SO MANY, TOO NUMEROUS TO LIST. I HAVE HAD SO MANY PEOPLE AS WELL AS PROPHETS COMPARE ME TO MARY (MOTHER OF JESUS); AND WRITING THIS BOOK AND GETTING YOUR WORD OUT THERE IS NOTHING SHORT OF A MIRACLE! TO WHOM MUCH IS GIVEN, MUCH IS REQUIRED AND YOU HAVE GIVEN ME MUCH, TO SAY THE LEAST!

IF I TRIED TO RECITE ALL YOUR WONDERFUL DEEDS, I WOULD NEVER COME TO THE END OF THEM. THANK YOU, FATHER, FOR TAKING THE FOOLISH THINGS OF THE WORLD TO CONFOUND THE WISE AND THE WEAK THINGS OF THE WORLD TO CONFOUND THE

ANN'S PRAYER TO THE ALMIGHTY

STRONG. THANK YOU, LORD, FOR TAKING THIS MESS (ME) AND MAKING ME YOUR MESSENGER."

Thank you, Lord!

"If I have found favor in your sight and I have been pleasing in your eyes and if this seems like the right thing to do, Father God, here I am like a little child who does not know my way around but here I am in the midst of writing this great book. I ask that you grant me this one wish and it is for you to give me the knowledge and the wisdom and sharp discernment to help your people. Help me, God, to let your wisdom guide my thoughts and my actions concerning your people all the days of my life." Father, help me to say what only you say, and to do what only you tell me to do!

Lord, as your people and all of your creation read my book, give them sharp discernment, wisdom and revelation that these dreams are indeed from you and this word or shall I say this compelling message has come at a critical and a crucial time. Do not let them dismiss what I believe, Father, what you have asked me to say! Comfort their hearts and let them know that they do not need to be afraid of these end time events if they are your children! I know that the storm will come but I pray that your people will not focus on it but will focus on "YOU." Father cause your people to draw from the strength of the future for we know what the future holds. We win!

◄ TOUCH NOT MY ANOINTED

Keep them from harm, Father, and protect them in time of trouble."

I love you!

My beautiful mother-Tennie M. Cannon.

Me and my dad-Willie Cannon.

When I was married to Kevin.

On our farm, we raised sheep.
I especially loved our baby lambs.

My sister Freda Cox and me.

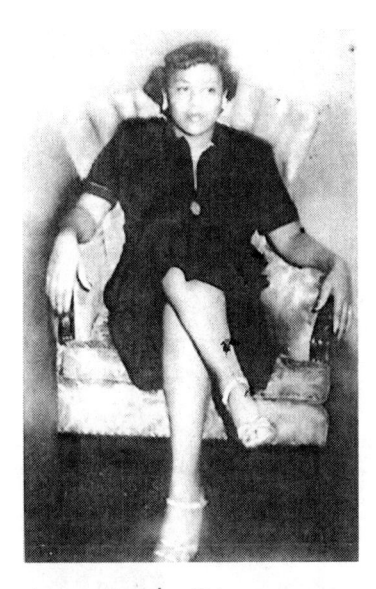

At my apartment in Okemos.

Aunt Freda Dixon, my mom's sister. (My sister Freda was named after her). After the tornado destroyed our home when I was small, we moved in with her and her family.

Jeanette Howard and me at the "Increase Event" Conference in Florida in 2011. This is where we both received a word from Myles Munroe.

My brother, Harvey, and his daughter, Octavia. Octavia (Tay) was almost a genius even at this age. I moved in with them when I first moved to Mich.

My favorite niece, Dr. Octavia (Tay) Cannon.

Me and my precious friend, Wendy.

◀ 284

My husband and me on our wedding day!

Larry and me at my birthday dinner.

Fast car but expensive upkeep. My dream car!